Each one of us knows what it is like to feel lonely, lost, and hopeless. The feeling of depression, although a very personal one, is an emotion we share with every other human being on this planet....

The mastering of depression enables us to accept more easily what otherwise would be overwhelming tragedy and also leads to greater maturity. As we accept some measure of depression, we accept some measure of reality, renouncing much of the magic of childish wishes.

In other words we have to learn how to "contain" a slight amount of depression to be happy. The more we can accept that a little depression is part of reality, the less depressed we are apt to be.
—Lucy Freeman

THE CRY FOR LOVE
was originally published by
The Macmillan Company.

Other books by Lucy Freeman

Fight Against Fears
Hope for the Troubled

Published by Pocket Books

 *Are there paperbound books you want
but cannot find in your retail stores?*

THE CRY FOR LOVE

Understanding & Overcoming Human Depression

LUCY FREEMAN

PUBLISHED BY POCKET BOOKS NEW YORK

THE CRY FOR LOVE

Macmillan edition published February, 1969
Pocket Book edition published June, 1970

Standard Book Number: 671-77189-2.
Library of Congress Catalog Card Number: 69-10316.

Printed in the U.S.A.

TO DR. SANDOR LORAND

*In tribute to
the contributions he has
made to the understanding
and treatment of depression*

Acknowledgment

Deepest thanks go to Mary Heathcote, Carl Morse and Richard Marek for their valuable help in putting this book together. Thanks also go to Dr. Rhoda Lorand and Dr. Walter A. Stewart for helpful suggestions, and other psychoanalysts who gave special interviews, all of whom are mentioned in the text.

Contents

I

×>×<×>×<×>×<×>×<×>×<×>×<×

The Experience
of Depression

1

><><><><><><><><><><><><><><><><><><><><><><><><><><

Depression: Description, Range and Symptoms in Everyday Life

Each one of us knows what it is like to feel lonely, lost and hopeless. The feeling of depression, although a very personal one, is an emotion we share with every other human being on this planet, be he a witch doctor in Rhodesia or a broker on Wall Street.

Even the President of the United States (or perhaps *especially* the President of the United States) has moods of depression. According to one of his staff, President Johnson "hated to be alone," battled continually against "the inherent loneliness of his position" and was a very restless man.

The entire country is suffering "a depression in the national spirit" according to the National Committee for an Effective Congress. This is a nonpartisan organization that tries to improve the quality of the government by supporting candidates for the House and Senate who take positions that transcend local and special interests.

As part of a report analyzing the first session of the 90th Congress, which ended December 15, 1967, the Committee stated: "America has experienced two great internal crises in her history: the Civil War and the Economic Depression of the 1930s. The country may now be on the brink of a third trauma, a depression of the national spirit."

It said, " 'Malaise,' 'frustration,' 'alienation,' 'identity' are now becoming part of the professional political vocabulary. At all levels of American life, people share similar fears, insecurities and gnawing doubts to such an intense degree that the country may in fact be suffering from a kind of national nervous breakdown." The war for control of outer space and the situation in Vietnam were mentioned as possible causes.

It is amazing how the feeling of depression has permeated the songs of our times. In the 1930s and 1940s, there was an occasional "My Man's Gone," "Am I Blue?" and "Melancholy Baby." But recently one jukebox held the following titles: "Depressed Feeling," "Free Again," "Dr. Feelgood," "Born to Lose," "My World Is Caving In," "Make the World Go Away," "Five Miles from Home," "The Beginning of Loneliness," "Here Comes the Morning," "Don't Sleep in the Subway," "Don't Ever Tell Me Good-bye," "The Tracks of My Tears," "Which Way to Nowhere," "Town Without Pity," and "Letter to John."

Literally speaking, what do we mean by "depression"? Webster defines it as "an emotional condition either normal or pathological, characterized by discouragement, a feeling of inadequacy, etc."

Thus the range of depression is wide—from "normal" to "pathological." It can vary from a fleeting, momentary mood of sadness to an intense, persistent conviction of worthlessness and hatred of self.

The very depressed person lacks self-esteem, suffers the tortures of the damned at the slightest of rebuffs either from someone he loves or an utter stranger. He acts as though all the world's injustices were aimed solely at his beleaguered head. He has difficulty making peace with himself or anyone else. Nothing seems to bring him pleasure. He blames others for his unhappiness. No matter how you try to please him, his answer is apt to be "Thanks a lot! For nothing." It is as though you cannot possibly make up to him for what he has lost.

This is quite a different state from falling prey to moods which last only a few hours, at the most a few days. These moods are easily shaken off by a cheerful word from someone you love, or by several martinis, a steak, a funny movie or perhaps eight hours of solid sleep. Or even by asking, "Why am I feeling blue? Life isn't so grim. Others have it far worse."

Reading about a stranger's misfortune—his sudden death in an automobile accident or from an overdose of sleeping pills, or his loss of thousands of dollars at the hands of a jewel thief—may lift us out of depression. We feel better by simply realizing we have escaped such fate.

Some people read obituaries of those they do not even know just to feel that at least it is something to remain alive no matter how many conflicts weigh down the soul.

TIMES OF DEPRESSION

There is, thus, vast difference between the sadness one feels when troubles are real and a general, pervasive depression that stems from vague, shadowy causes. Under certain conditions it is normal to be sad.

When someone we love dies we would, indeed, be unnatural if we did not feel bereaved, an emotion which carries with it some feeling of depression.

There are other times it is natural to feel depressed at certain events or crises. One would be a dreamer or a clown not to be sad at the end of a love affair. It is even possible to die of a broken heart, according to recent studies of a psychiatrist, Dr. Murray Parkes, of the Tavistock Institute of Human Relations in London. He reported, after studying widowers, that the depression of a man after the death of his wife greatly increases his chance of death during his first six months as a widower. He held that grief aggravates illnesses, particularly heart ailments, and thus could lead to death. The heart disease death rate for widowers over fifty-five within six months of losing their wives was 47 per cent higher than for those whose wives were still alive.

"Call it grief, or a broken heart, or whatever you want," he commented, "but my studies show that bereavement is definitely a cause of death."

The end of a marriage, or separation either temporary or permanent from someone to whom we have become attached, may seem for the moment like the end of the world. So may the loss of a job, or a large amount of money in the stock market or in a business, or even at the racetrack.

An unfair tongue-lashing by an employer or the failure of someone to keep an important appointment may lead to temporary depression. A child may feel depressed if he believes he has been scolded unjustly by a parent. Or a parent may feel depressed if he believes a child rebels without cause.

There are certain times in life when a woman may feel depressed, such as menopause, which implies to many women a goodbye to youth and femininity. Depression has been so prevalent after babies that the phrase "postpartum blues" is now part of our language. Women experience a letdown, a feeling of having lost something, in sharp contrast to the feeling of joy and happiness they possessed while pregnant.

Women also may become depressed monthly at the time of menstruation although psychoanalysts tell us this does not need to be. The depression may be caused by a number of unconscious conflicts including the wish to be a man and resentment at being a woman which is brought into sharp realization once a month. Many women, however, expect to feel blue at this time, prepare for the depression and know it will lift in three or four days.

A single girl may feel depressed because she finds herself alone weekend after weekend, determined she is not going to face the torture of spending weekends with friends who are married and have countless little children who wake her early on the one morning she can sleep late. Underneath such feelings of depression may lie her unconscious resentment at not having a family of her own.

The weather may set off a depression. On a wet, gray day, we may feel as though the gloom and the sadness of the skies mirror our inner mood. As the rain ceases or the fog lifts, so does our depression.

Through the ages there seems to be some mysterious connection between depression, madness and a full moon. Milton spoke of:

> *Demoniac frenzy, moping melancholy,*
> *And moon-struck madness.*

The full moon is supposed to bring on moods of madness. Some police records show that crimes of violence and passion increase when the moon is full.

"Blue Monday," which beckons us back to work, ending the weekend of play, depresses some, although every day is blue if you feel very depressed. Dr. Sandor Ferenczi, friend and colleague of Freud's, noted that many of his patients became depressed on Sundays. He theorized that a large number of people are able to ward off the outbreak of "severe neurotic symptoms" only by working at high pressure. Their psychic equilibrium, maintained by constant work, is overthrown in the course of a Sunday or holiday or a longer period of inactivity, he said. They feel better again only as they resume work.

"Work in ever-increasing dosage becomes as indispensable to them as the habitual drug to the morphine addict," he claimed. He added that there is in such people, as a result of too severe a repression of their instincts, "a constant danger of depression."

Holidays bring depression to some. People who find themselves alone and think of everyone else as being with families and having fun grow dispirited. It is not unusual for some lonely old lady or man to hurl himself out of the window of a drab hotel room on New Year's Eve. Spring and summer are supposed to be times of enjoyment and yet there are those who grow most depressed then because they have no one with whom to share pleasure.

Some are depressed every morning, not able to wake until they have sleepily consumed three or four cups of coffee. Others find it impossible to go to bed at night, depressed after coping with the day's petty chores, and go in search of excitement as one of the "night people."

There are those who are depressed if they do not compulsively observe certain toilet habits every day. If they fail to do so, they feel "bad" and "wicked" and sink into a black mood.

Some find themselves depressed when they live alone, others when they live with someone they do not love. Although you may be married, with five children cavorting around you, you may feel just as lonely as if you dwelled by yourself.

The depression that follows isolation can be seen in the extreme in men who must spend long hours alone in outer space or in remote parts of the earth. Antarctica is the scene of an interesting study being conducted by a research team led by Dr. Jay T. Shurley and Dr. Chester M. Pierce, psychiatrists at the University of Oklahoma Medical Center. They are trying to find out what happens psychologically to twenty-one men forced to live for a year in the isolation and cold of a research station deep under the ice and snow at the South Pole. Previous studies have shown that humans forced to live in prolonged and confined isolation frequently undergo severe emotional problems, including extreme depression, feelings of irritability, hopelessness, inability to concentrate and insomnia.

SIGNS OF DEPRESSION

People evidence depression in many ways. The feeling of boredom, either with the self or someone else, may be one sign of feeling depressed. Often we are bored with those who arouse in us reminders of conflicts within that we wish to hide from our own awareness.

Another common sign of depression may be the inability to go to sleep, or to wake up at three or four every morning, unable to fall asleep again. At these moments the most embarrassing, shameful and humiliating experiences of our lives are likely to erupt into consciousness as we lie in misery hating ourselves more and more.

Some show their depression by letting their appearance deteriorate, not caring how they look. Cleanliness may suffer when it is an effort to bathe or brush the teeth. A dentist told one man to brush his teeth three times daily and a fourth time, too, if he could squeeze it in.

"Four times!" wailed the man. "It's all I can do to push the toothbrush across my mouth once in the morning."

Some openly display their depression, caught in a web of apathy. They are physically and emotionally weary, hardly able to get through the day. Others mask depression by bustling activity and restlessness.

There are those who brood and those who try to hide sadness with laughter. But usually the latter can keep up the denial only so long before the depression within erupts in one way or another.

Like every other emotion of which we are capable, depression is natural when it occurs moderately and occasionally. If we did not know despair, we would not know joy. Only by experiencing emotions that are opposite does each hold meaning. Incidentally, depression is not the same as feeling the need for solitude, which enables us to escape temporarily from the turmoil around us, to rest for the moment and renew psychic energy.

At times children may be greater realists than adults. A little girl of eight approached a psychoanalyst who was visiting her parents and asked, "What exactly do you do?"

Trying to explain in terms of her understanding, he said, "Let's pretend you're me, the doctor, and I'm the patient. I come to you and say, 'Doctor, can you help me? I feel so low, so unhappy, so depressed.' "

The little girl looked at him, shrugged her shoulders philosophically and said, "So?"

Depression is dangerous only when it exists in extreme degree and stops us from working or loving or wanting to keep alive. That is, when it drives us to suicidal thoughts or into a state of inertia. The latter feeling appears in catatonia, where the man, woman or child will not muster enough energy to move, even to speak.

As Thomas Mann so perceptively put it in *The Magic Mountain,* speech "is civilization itself. The word, even the most contradictory word, preserves contact—it is silence which isolates."

When we are depressed in a mild way we may experience how the very depressed person feels in more intense fashion. At such a time we feel unloved, unlovable and incapable of loving. We may, for the moment, wonder why we were born, what purpose there is in remaining alive one second longer.

When it is excessive, depression may slowly destroy a person. As Freud said, "Every excess contains within it the germs of its own decay."

At the other extreme of the normal depression is the psychotic despair of the man or woman who must be placed in a mental hospital to keep from killing himself. Authorities differ as to whether all states, from the slight to the most severe depression, are a matter of degree, or whether the neurotic depression and the psychotic depression are completely different.

The very depressed person wants to isolate himself from the world so others cannot hurt him and he cannot hurt others. He tries to become, as Henry Murray, psychoanalyst, says, "dead to the outer world" and "dead to the inner world." The most extreme form of isolation, suicide, makes him dead literally to both outer and inner world.

Depression, in its extreme, is a feeling of helplessness in the face of overwhelming burden. This burden of psychic pain, in Freud's words, appears to "empty the ego." The pain precedes the depression and the depression itself is pain.

Dr. Philippe Pinel, the famous French psychiatrist who brought about reforms in mental hospitals (then called lunatic asylums) at the turn of the nineteenth century, stated that the signs generally shown in depression were "taciturnity, a thoughtful, pensive air, gloomy suspicions and a love of solitude." He added:

Those traits, indeed, appear to distinguish the characters of some men otherwise in good health, and frequently in prosperous circumstances. Nothing, however, can be more hideous than the figure of a melancholic, brooding over his imaginary misfortunes. If, moreover, possessed of power, and endowed with a perverse disposition and a sanguinary heart, the image is rendered still more repulsive.

The very depressed person feels useless, finds it difficult to concentrate, cannot relax, cannot "get going." He thinks life is "just too much," feels tired even though he has energy, doesn't know what he really wants. He has little sense of belonging to anyone or anything or any place, is easily hurt, easily discouraged and troubled by occasional thoughts of going crazy. He feels guilty but doesn't know why.

He is also apt to feel crippled sexually. Depression tends to lower sexual desire so that the person is not interested in sex, or, when he does take part, feels unfulfilled. A number of men and women speak of being depressed after sexual intimacy. Freud noted, "For in spite of everything each sexual satisfaction always involves a reduction in sexual over-estimation . . . It is the fate of sensual love to become extinguished when it is satisfied; for it to be able to last, it must from the first be mixed with purely tender components."

He was referring to the idealization that occurs when we fall "madly" or "desperately" in love, a time when sensual impulses override reason. If gripped by desperate emotions we may be depressed after sex, even though we may engage in it often, because the feeling of tenderness is absent.

A recent study aimed at describing the differences between various kinds of depressions was conducted at the Institute for Psychosomatic and Psychiatric Research and Training of the Michael Reese Hospital and Medical Center in Chicago. An attempt was made to survey a group of depressed patients with the purpose of reporting differences in the pattern of their illness, their personality before depression set in and how the depressive process works.

Five main characteristics emerged, according to the

researchers.[1] These five characteristics (some patients possessed more than one) were:

1. Characteristics of hopelessness, helplessness, failure, sadness, unworthiness, guilt and internal suffering, with a pronounced self-concept of "badness."

2. Characteristics of concern with material loss and an inner conviction that this feeling (and the illness) could be changed if only the outside world would provide something.

3. Characteristics of guilt over wrongdoings, wishes to make restitution and a feeling that the illness was brought on by the person himself and is deserved.

4. Characteristics of "free anxiety."

5. Characteristics of envy, loneliness, martyred affliction, attempts to provoke the world into making redress, and a gratification from the illness.

Each of the main groups of characteristics "describe different aspects or facets of a similar process," according to Dr. Julian Miller, one of the researchers.

The first group, Dr. Miller pointed out, describes primarily those with an "inner sense of badness and suffering." The second describes those "who can project onto the outside world the responsibility for their own inner feelings." The third group describes persons with "characteristics of guilt that are much more intense openly and accompanied by wishes to make restitution." The fourth, "free anxiety," is characteristic of "some of the patients who were depressed"; the fifth group "describes the martyred, lonely, envious patient openly obtaining a great deal of secondary gain from the illness and attempting to provoke guilt in others and by such manipulation to force them to do what the patient wants."

This study focused on the severely depressed, but in lesser degree, the characteristics may be present in those we might think of as the normally depressed.

There is, as mentioned in the final group of characteristics, a sense of wanting to provoke others into making redress. Depression may be, in part, "a game, a manipulation, a maneuver," in the words of Daniel A. Sugarman, a psychologist who has treated the depressed person. The latter tries to persuade others to play his sad game of downsmanship as he lists his woes in an effort to enlist their sympathy. He does not even care if he gets contempt, for "even contempt is better than nothing—any kind of attention, even a beating, is better than nothing at all," says Dr. Sugarman.

But the depressed person is not likely to get the company he desperately craves because depression comes across to others as a form of selfishness and cruelty. It is as though the depressed person blames *you* for his depression and expects *you* to pull him out of it. He does not get much pleasure from life nor is he able to give much pleasure. Therefore, it is painful to be near him, for he is no fun, no challenge; his imagination is throttled. In everyday existence we tend to shun the depressed person, who may find it difficult even to discover somebody in his office with whom to lunch.

Yet we realize he is suffering, that the depression arises from forces within himself that he cannot control, and part of our heart goes out to him.

In one sense, depression is a plea for comfort and solace. A child's scream brings him help. But an adult is not allowed to scream; if he does, he is taken away and locked up. Thus his depression is his silent scream.

WAYS OF FIGHTING DEPRESSION

Perhaps it might not be too fanciful to say that the Number 1 killer in the nation is not heart failure or high blood pressure or highway crashes but the emotion that may lie at the root of all these—depression.

We might even call depression the Number 1 killer of the world, in that war could be described as a universal psychic depression. War stands for despair; it represents a giving-up of faith in man's ability to use his reason in coping with hate. War means resorting to the jungle expedient of wantonly murdering other men as a way of settling quarrels.

For the individual human being, depression may have

crippling effects on both mind and body, which range from partial disabling to complete disabling—death.

It may seem paradoxical, but it is nonetheless true that depression may be both a savior and a killer. We may unconsciously use it to save ourselves from what we believe a worse fate, and we may also try to fight it with weapons that wind up as boomerangs.

One of the most popular weapons used against depression may be physical illness. We learn as children the efficacy of illness as a way of getting special concern, attention and care from those we love. It is not strange that later, when we feel in need of affection and attention, we may unconsciously choose to fall ill.

An underlying depression may be masked by physical illnesses of various types. "Conversion" is the name Freud used to describe the transformation of psychic distress into physical symptoms.

It now appears that even the common cold may be a way of fighting depression, a fact psychoanalysts have long suspected. A study of patients showed that underlying certain colds were depressive symptoms, according to Dr. Bruce Ruddick.[2] These colds followed the loss of or separation from someone important to the one who caught cold. The cold represented an unconscious attempt to regain the lost person by psychically incorporating him through the respiratory system, specifically the mouth and nose.

Dr. Ruddick pointed out that the word "cold" in other languages was associated with the words for death, birth, pregnancy and sexual arousal. Anthropologists have found the use of smells prevalent in some cultures to ward off the return of ghosts following someone's death. The air was believed to carry ghosts and also, among some primitive peoples, to carry the seeds by which babies were conceived. Around this fantasy theories of conception, life and death were elaborated upon (including the fantasy that the "air" carries the germs that cause a cold, or that cold air causes colds).

Dr. Leon Saul found that the common cold occurred in patients as a result of unconscious emotional conflicts. He suggested that the feeling of fatigue and loss of energy so frequently associated with colds was a sign of depression rather than a toxic effect.

A three-year study of ten patients who caught thirty-five colds was reported by Dr. Merl M. Jackel.[3] In only one instance was the evidence of depression "not clear." Most of the depression centered on the loss of someone. Dr. Jackel stated, "It is my impression that the most consistent finding associated with the Common Cold is the emotion of depression. . . . In my opinion, the Common Cold is the result of psychophysiological changes which accompany depressions in certain individuals."

The relationship between depression and the common cold was also reported in a study conducted by scientists at the Great Lakes Naval Medical Research Unit and Cornell Medical School. They deliberately exposed a group of volunteers to live cold viruses. Only those men struggling with feelings of depression, anger and frustration in their personal lives caught cold. The virus had no effect on the others.

As everyone knows who has had a cold (which means everyone), whether or not it is caused by depression, it can make you feel depressed. Some get as near to suicide or murder when they suffer the common cold as at any other time, even when there may be no more provocation than a stuffy nose.

However, the physical illness used against depression may take any form—dizziness, fatigue, headaches, stomach-aches, ache in muscles, constipation, diarrhea, chest pains, skin rashes, overall feeling of weakness, pain in the lungs or heart.

Cancer and the emotions have been linked by Dr. David M. Kissen, director of the Psychosomatic Research Unit of the Southern General Hospital in Glasgow, Scotland. He studied 366 lung cancer patients and a control group of 366 persons who smoked but did not have cancer. He reported that the cancer victims tended to have poor emotional outlets, had been forced to cope with unhappy personal situations and, in general, suppressed their feelings.

One recent study in this country showed that of 500 men and women who were depressed, 74 per cent first consulted general practitioners and specialists for physical ailments, before seeking psychological help. These 500 saw a total of 1278 physicians, most of whom did not ask about their emotional state. Of the 500, 87 per cent were given a medical diagnosis. The underlying depression was recognized at the time of their first visit in only 47 of the 500 patients.

But doctors are becoming more aware of the connection between depression and physical illness. Two thirds of all Americans now consult doctors for ailments that have emotional rather than physical origin, according to Dr. Augustus Gibson, vice president and director of the Schering Corporation.[4] Some physicians have put this figure as high as 80 to 90 per cent.

Most patients seeking general practitioners complain of physical pain *and* feelings of helplessness, unhappiness, sorrow, self-depreciation and loneliness. They are able to carry on daily work although the depression slows them down and affects the quality of what they do. There is the businessman with ulcers who describes how he just missed a big deal because he could not find the time to prepare properly for it, then confesses he has a mistress as well as a wife but doesn't really love either. There is the college student who suffers migraine headaches who says he would be getting A's instead of C's if he could only concentrate on his work instead of feeling so lonely away from home. There is the housewife who has arthritis and tells how exhausted she is by the demands of her three children.

The name "tired mother syndrome" has been pinned on a group of symptoms shown by weary young mothers, by Dr. Leonard L. Lovshin of the Cleveland Clinic Foundation. After studying forty-eight mothers complaining of chronic fatigue, he reported:

Most young mothers are tired. Seldom is this fatigue due to organic disease. There are just too many things for them to do in too short a time! In its most common form, the tired mother syndrome afflicts a worried, tense, overly-conscientious mother who cannot quite keep up with all the tasks she has set for herself. Despite laborsaving devices in the home, life has become more complicated, not less.

Because of their chronic tiredness, some women turn into nags and scream at their husband and children. Others become physically ill and get a backache or hives or, most common of all, a nervous tension headache. In reviewing the history of one thousand headache patients, Dr. Arnold P. Friedman noted that two out of three sufferers were women.[5]

Illness is not the only weapon used against depression. In fact, almost anything we do may be used; rather, anything we overdo or underdo. Some try to combat it by plunging into sleep, needing ten or twelve hours each night. Others cannot sleep at all, toss away the desperate hours. Some try to fill every single moment with work. Others cannot work at all; their minds and limbs paralyzed, they retreat to bed or sit glumly all day in a chair. One of the most popular ways of trying to avoid depression is by compulsively watching television or listening to the radio.

Sexual activity may reflect a fight against depression. (As one psychoanalyst said, "Sex runs through everything.") Some completely lose interest in sex, others indulge in it endlessly and aimlessly, finding in the momentary closeness to another body a brief respite from depression.

Some refuse to smoke at all; others are driven to chain smoking. Some lose their appetite; others cannot stop eating. Food is a major weapon against depression, as people eat for solace. The phrase "hidden hunger" was coined to describe an appetite that is not normal but excessive, caused by emotional conflicts.

The hostess who sneaks into the kitchen when the guests are not looking and stuffs into her mouth an extra slice of chocolate cake or snatches a spoonful of cold mashed potatoes is a victim of hidden hunger. As is the boy who heads for the refrigerator after his father has spoken sharply to him about his homework.

One woman found that when her husband left for work each morning she would eat a second breakfast, as a result of which she was putting on unwanted pounds. She finally realized there were things she wanted to say to her husband at the breakfast table, but she did not dare talk because he was always irritable early in the morning. Instead, she swallowed her words, felt depressed, then consumed a double portion of food. The added weight made her feel additionally depressed.

Bizarre eating habits in thirteen children were studied by Dr. Gerald F. Powell of Duke University Medical Center. The children, ranging in age from 3½ to 11½, were only half as tall as they should have been for their age. Although they were well fed at mealtimes, they ate almost constantly, raiding refrigerators and eating whole jars of mustard and mayonnaise and whole loaves of bread, stealing from the plates of their brothers and sisters, sometimes even digging in garbage cans for leftovers or eating what lay in the cat or dog's dish. They were also always thirsty.

As soon as the children were placed in a convalescent hospital they began to grow, even though they received neither growth hormones nor psychiatric help. The abnormal eating habits disappeared at once, the children appeared happier and less withdrawn.

"The unusual eating and drinking habits suggest emotional disturbances in the children and abnormal home environments," said Dr. Powell. "In some way, their emotions affected the output of their growth hormones."

Although some of the children continued to change for the better after returning home, several had to go back to the hospital when growth again stopped.

Dr. Powell found there were, indeed, "abnormal home environments." Five sets of parents were either divorced or separated. "Marital strife of a marked degree" existed in two more families. Four fathers drank excessively and five were indulging in affairs. Most of the fathers spent little time at home. In no instance had the father given much time to his child. All the fathers had "noticeably bad tempers."

"Maternal love was more difficult to evaluate." Though the mothers were interviewed often, they usually provided information about the behavior of their husbands "but little about themselves."

We might guess that the mothers were also quite emotionally disturbed, especially those with alcoholic husbands, for the woman who chooses to remain with an alcoholic is apt to have deep conflicts of her own but can blame all on the more obvious problems of her husband.

Alcoholism is another way of trying to fight off depression, in that it temporarily makes the drinker unaware of his frustration as he blots out his problems. One sociologist, Dr. Ira H. Cisin of George Washington University, recently estimated that between four and five million Americans are "problem drinkers" who cannot leave alcohol alone and are harmed by it. He noted further that more women were taking to drink as they achieved "first-class citizenship" with men. The women, however, are "very light drinkers" (among male imbibers 21 per cent are "heavy drinkers," among female, only 5 per cent) and only 60 per cent of women drink, compared with 77 per cent of men.

Then there are those who take to pills, either to give them more energy or put them to sleep, or both. Some consume pep pills during the day, sleeping pills at night.

Auden called this the age of anxiety but it also might be called the age of the anti-depressant pill. The Food and Drug Administration reports that more than twice as much barbituric acid derivatives (which go into sleeping pills and tranquilizers) is produced every year in the United States than would be required to kill every man, woman and child in the nation—a total of 1,000,000 pounds of barituric acid derivatives and 100,000 pounds of amphetamine and methamphetamine products.

Thousands daily try to combat depression by popping a

little pill into their mouths—4,000,000 persons annually, according to estimates by physicians, buy pills without prescription at drug stores. In addition there are 6,000,000 more men and women given pills on the recommendation of physicians in their offices, or in mental hospitals. Thus a total of 10,000,000, or 5 per cent of our population (and this is a conservative estimate), depend on the magic of pills to do away with feelings of sadness and gloom.

Sometimes the magic potion turns into poison, as in the case of the manager of the world-famous Beatles, Brian Epstein. Found dead in his bed at his London home on August 27, 1967, his death was ruled "accidental," according to *The New York Times* account. The coroner reported it had been caused by an "incautious self-overdosage" of the sleeping drug Carbrital. Dr. Robert Donald Teare, a pathologist, said at the inquest he found traces of an anti-depressant drug, barbiturate and bromide in Mr. Epstein's blood. Dr. Norman Cowan, Mr. Epstein's physician for three years, declared he had prescribed anti-depressant and hypnotic drugs for Mr. Epstein, who suffered from "insomnia, anxiety and depression."

It is interesting to note that in studies conducted on placebos (pills with no medication, usually containing just sugar) there is a high spontaneous rate of improvement for depressed persons. Nine separate studies showed that more than half of those given the sugar pills improved in two to six weeks. Psychiatrists believe it is the act of the doctor giving his time, attention and care, rather than the pill itself, that is responsible for many an improved mood—"Somebody cares about me, so the world looks brighter."

Then there are the country's 700,000 drug addicts, known to be among the most depressed of humans, according to psychiatrists who have tried to help them. The addict is one of the most difficult of all to treat because his depression runs so deep.

The drug addict is different from the alcoholic in that he is breaking a law. The alcoholic, when he purchases liquor, is doing so with the sanction of the government. This means the addict is more rebellious and cares even less about himself and others than the alcoholic.

The smoking of marijuana has been increasing so rapidly among teen-agers that it is now a major hazard to public health and law enforcement. It "has become the way to gain social acceptance," declared Thomas A. Facelle, Jr., senior assistant district attorney of Westchester County. "No longer is any stigma attached to it. When we talk to youngsters about drug addiction their attitude is, 'it doesn't apply to me because I just smoke marijuana.' "[6]

County executive Edwin G. Michaelian pointed out, as many authorities have, that "the use of marijuana is vicious. Youths start on it and then invariably turn to LSD and heroin."

According to Walter Panas, former president of the Westchester Superintendents Association, "Marijuana is a plague-like disease, slowly but surely strangling our young people."

There is an increasing amount of deaths among hippies from the use of LSD and other drugs. Hospitals in New York City, for instance, report a growing number of such deaths as young men and women are brought in by ambulance too late to be saved.

Another way men and women seek relief from depressed feelings is by taking to the highway, sometimes causing death on the road. More than half the seventy-two drivers responsible for fatal accidents in Washtenaw County (the county in which Ann Arbor, Michigan, is located) from October 29, 1961, to December 31, 1964, were suffering from some form of mental disturbance.[7]

At least 58 per cent of these drivers had classifiable psychiatric illness. An even larger proportion were involved, at the time of the fatal crash, in some serious personal crisis, such as difficulty with a husband or wife, pressure on the job or financial worries.

Of the drivers studied, twenty-nine were confirmed alcoholics and exactly 50 per cent had a serious drinking problem, according to Dr. Melvin L. Selzer. He emphasized that the great hazard in our serious highway accidents is not the social drinker who is only slightly intoxicated, but the chronic alcoholic.

Dr. Selzer observed:

The automobile lends itself admirably to attempts at self-destruction because of the frequency of its use, the generally accepted inherent hazards of driving, and the fact that it offers the individual an opportunity to imperil or end his life without consciously confronting himself with his suicidal intent.

The automobile presents the depressed and frustrated individual with an opportunity to end his life in what he may perceive as a burst of glory. The automobile may also constitute a special enticement to the aggressive and vengeful feelings present in any would-be suicide.

The extreme in depression is suicide. There appear to be few cases of suicide or suicide attempts where the person was not very depressed immediately preceding the act.

Suicide is the Number 3 killer between the ages of twenty and thirty-five in this country and the Number 10 killer for all age groups. Severe depression has caused an estimated two million persons now alive to try suicide at one time or another, including a number of children. Depression annually causes about twenty-two thousand "known" suicides and an estimated forty thousand more that are covered up in the records by police, families and physicians.

Dr. Karl Menninger makes the point that there are more suicides annually than murders—every twenty-four minutes somewhere in the United States someone takes his own life.[8] Dr. Menninger speaks of the taboo that exists in connection with suicide, which, he says, is related to strongly repressed emotions.

"People do not like to think seriously and factually about suicide," he states.

He notes that mystery, murder and detective stories are turned out "by the thousands" in which "the obvious explanation is pierced by the subtle persistency of the hero-sleuth," but "it is almost never the explanation of a *suicide* which is sought in these stories, but that of a *murder."*

He refers to the "glib explanations" offered as to the cause of suicides in the daily newspapers, in life-insurance reports, on death certificates and in statistical surveys. Suicide, according to these, is the "simple and logical consequence of ill health, discouragement, financial reverses, humiliation, frustration or unrequited love."

What amazes him, he says, is not that these simple explanations are continually offered but that they are so readily and unquestioningly accepted "in a world where science and everyday experience alike confirm the untrustworthiness of the obvious." He adds, "No such credulity or lack of curiosity exists, for example, with reference to the motives for murder."

Statistics show that suicide is more frequent in spring than in any other season. It is more frequent among single than married persons, more common in city than in country areas and occurs more often in peace than in war.

For every completed suicide there are between eight and ten times as many suicide attempts which fail, or about 250,000 a year, it is estimated. Young women account for two thirds of the attempts, which suggests how devastated they feel when rejected by a suitor or abandoned by a husband. Many women apparently do not care to live if they do not have a man. Or perhaps their attempt to kill themselves is a desperate gesture to bring back the rejecting man by arousing his guilt and remorse.

Although more women than men try suicide, more men succeed. Men outnumber the women two to one in actual suicides. The man between the ages of twenty-five and thirty-four appears the most vulnerable. One out of every thirteen deaths in this age group was reported as suicide in 1960, a ratio considerably higher than any other age group. We may hazard a guess that establishing himself as an adult sexually and as a breadwinner can be even more overwhelming to the troubled man than rejection in love is to the troubled woman.

As a rule, suicides make headlines only when the person is prominent. That having money, or being famous, is no deterrent to killing oneself becomes evident when we read about those with wealth and fame who nevertheless, put a bullet through their brain, take an overdose of sleeping pills or jump off tall buildings without any apparent reason. There are always reasons, of course; it is just that no one knows them.

Sometimes the reasons given seem ludicrous, as Dr Menninger says. Some were shocked by the stated cause of the suicide of Alain Zick, chef of the Relais de Porquerolles in Paris, who killed himself with a shotgun on September 22, 1966. He committed suicide, according to the newspapers, because the *Guide Michelin,* the social register of gastronomy in France, not only stripped the famous restaurant, noted for its bouillabaisse, of its two stars (meaning "excellent cuisine, worth a detour"), but removed it entirely from the book. We can imagine how troubled a man Alain Zick must have been for this psychic straw to cause him to take his life.

Murder, as has often been said, is a form of suicide. The one who kills knows it will mean his own death or lifelong imprisonment, a kind of death.

The close tie between murder and suicide, and the depression that may underlie murder, was shown by Charles J. Whitman, the architecture student who slaughtered sixteen people on August 1, 1966, as he fired from the tower of the University of Texas in Austin. Whitman telegraphed his intention to commit both murder and suicide in several ways.

For one, he left notes that revealed he did not intend to be taken alive, that he planned to keep on killing until he himself was killed. For another, just before the mass murder, he sought an interview with Dr. Maurice D. Heatly, staff psychiatrist at the university, on the recommendation of a general physician whom he had consulted for headaches. Whitman told Dr. Heatly he was possessed by an urge to "go up on the tower with a deer rifle and start shooting people." He spoke with deep hatred of his father (whom he despised "with mortal passion," according to one of his notes). He also showed signs of weeping, according to Dr. Heatly's report. After this session, Dr. Heatly made a second appointment for the following week but Whitman never returned.

According to *The New York Times* report in the notes he wrote on his worn portable typewriter before he went out to kill, addressed "to whom it may concern," Whitman spoke of being sick of the world, said it was not worth living in and that he wanted to get away from it. To his friends over the years he had presented "a happy, cheerful face," but Kathy, the wife he killed, along with his mother, had told some friends her husband often suffered such fits of depression that she was afraid to leave him alone.

How often it appears in our newspapers that a man who suddenly "goes berserk" and murders his family or a string of strangers is described by those who thought they knew him as "a nice, gentle, considerate man." Murders committed by those who have suppressed their aggressive instincts over the years outnumber by more than three to one murders committed by those who have shown outward hostility, according to George R. Bach, psychologist with the Institute for Group Psychotherapy in Beverly Hills.[9]

Most of us fortunately are not a Whitman, who killed and then was killed, or a Marilyn Monroe, who put an end to her unhappiness with an overdose of sleeping pills. But one reason we read with horror and yet perhaps also with fascination of such tragic deeds is that there lies within us the same capacity to kill—ourselves and others.

Upon seeing criminals taken to the gallows in the middle of the sixteenth century, John Bradford exclaimed, "But for the grace of God there goes John Bradford." Most of us can thank the grace of God, or whomever we choose, that our depressions are not so crippling as to drive us to murder or suicide.

2

<hr>

Fantasy and Depression

We live in two worlds, the world of reality and the world of fantasy. The world of reality we share with others. The world of fantasy is our own private, inner world.

The depressed person is apt to live too completely in his world of fantasy. For him, the real world is so painful that he retreats to a world in which fantasy reigns supreme.

The human mind is capable of two kinds of fantasy, as Freud discovered—conscious and unconscious. The daydreams and wishes of which we are aware constitute our conscious fantasies. The wishes and thoughts of which we are not aware make up our unconscious fantasies.

Fantasy, both conscious and unconscious, is a psychic mechanism for the protection of the self. The ability to indulge in fantasy takes the edge off psychic and physiological pain.

As children we may have learned to act in certain ways to conform to the orders of our parents and that vague, ephemeral whipping boy, "society." But in fantasy we may concoct whatever script we please, direct all the actors, produce the play, select the audience, even write the reviews.

In the purest sense of the word, fantasy pertains to a picture in the mind. The word "fantasy" comes from the Greek phantasia, the look or appearance of a thing. Its literal translation means "a making visible." Thus "seeing" is crucial to the original meaning. But that mean ing has been expanded to include not only the vision that whirls through our mind but the words we make up as we speak to ourselves or put words in the mouths of others. It also includes our random thoughts, which often, upon closer examination, prove not quite so random after all but purposeful in our psychic life.

Freud described fantasy as a way of thinking kept free from the testing of reality and which remains subordinated to the principle of getting pleasure out of life. Some fantasies are stimulated by our own mind, others by external stimulation and some by both external and internal. Any strong emotion that cannot be expressed in reality but which has a need for expression may stimulate a fantasy which serves as a partial expression, a substitute expression, of that emotion.

Fantasies have as their driving power unsatisfied wishes, Freud held. He said, "Every separate phantasy contains the fulfillment of a wish."[1]

The play of children is determined by their wishes, really by the child's *one* wish, Freud maintained, which is to be grown-up, the wish that helps to "bring him up." The child always plays at being grown-up; "in play he imitates what is known to him of the lives of adults."

But some of the wishes from which the fantasies of an adult spring "are such as have to be entirely hidden; therefore he is ashamed of his phantasies as being childish and as something prohibited."

We choose our daydreams, which usually we concoct to give us pleasure. But we have no control over our unconscious fantasies, which may reflect wishes not acceptable to the conscious part of our mind. Unconscious fantasies emerge in disguised form: for instance, in the stuff of dreams, which are so complicated that only a psychoanalyst, trained in the interpretation of dreams, can help us understand the many meanings of a dream.

According to Freud, who discovered the importance of fantasy life in determining how we act, and thus its role in depression, the conscious fantasies of an adult are his "castles in the air," his daydreams, similar to a child's

play. But while a child will talk freely about his fantasies
adults believe it is not "right" to confess daydreams. The
think they should be living completely in the world o
reality and are ashamed of daydreams.

"The adult cherishes them [his daydreams] as hi
most intimate possession and as a rule he would rathe
confess all his misdeeds than tell his daydreams," Freuc
declared.

But it is these very daydreams that enable many of u
to get through life without doing something we knov
would hurt us or those we love. Take the average man (i
there be such a creature except in fantasy). Nerves twang
ing from the blast of the alarm clock, he reluctantl
drags himself out of his rumpled bed each morning
dresses, gulps breakfast, rushes off to work, combats
competitive world, lurches homeward, bolts down suppe
and retreats to bed to await anew the alarm's assault.

The day and night are made more bearable, however
because of a slight amount of fantasy in which he permit
himself to indulge. Before the start of civilization's dail
demands, as our imaginary hero stands washing his fac
in the pink, purple and blue-wallpapered bathroom witl
matching flowered towels, he dashes cold water in hi
eyes to help clear away the debris of a dream in which h
swam thirty miles fighting a stormy, shark-infested ocean
after the ship of which he was admiral was torpedoed b
the enemy.

He shaves shakily, thinking, "If only I didn't have to g
to that boring office. I could sleep until noon, then hea
for the club and play a peaceful game of golf, no idio
Sunday amateurs slicing all over the course. If it rained,
could sit home and read *Remembrance of Things Past*
which I've been trying to get to for twenty years."

Wiping off the lather, he fantasizes, "I should hav
married a rich woman whose father died on our honey
moon and left us a million." He sighs, dreams on
"Maybe I could invent some little gadget that a woman
needs around the house. Say a dustcloth that she coulc
control with a push button as she sits in a chair anc
swivels and eats chocolates to her heart's content anc

watches *As the World Turns*. That would put me on Easy Street."

He stumbles into underwear, shirt, trousers, jacket, selects a tie, combs his hair and as he gazes at his image in the mirror thinks, "You're not so bad-looking, old boy, even after twelve years in chains. Maybe that babe on the train last night, giving you the eye across the aisle, was on the make. Wonder if she commutes every day? Must look for her tonight."

At the breakfast table he faces a wife who has tied around her like a burlap bag a purple dressing gown scarred with the brown of coffee stains. Her eyes barely focus as she stuporously hands him *The New York Times*. He thinks, "Wonder if old Ann knows she looks like the Witch of Endor in the morning? Sonya would never have let me see her like that. She was a charmer, even at 7 A.M. Wonder why I didn't marry her?"

He stares at his eleven-year-old daughter slurping away at Kellogg's Corn Flakes, her geography book propped in front of her as she studies the lesson she should have tackled the night before instead of gluing herself to another repeat of *Casablanca*. He thinks, "Undisciplined little brat. She'll be a beauty, though, one of these days, if she loses twenty pounds."

After breakfast, he kisses his wife goodbye, speeds to the suburban station in his Oldsmobile convertible, catches the train to the city. Ensconced on a rocklike, centuries-old plush seat, he opens the newspaper, reads the latest front-page arguments by the country's high officials for the continuation of the war in Vietnam, thinks, "It's all too much for me. They never tell us the truth, anyhow."

He turns to the obituary page, scans the headlines for a familiar name, finds none. He always reads every obituary, studying the ages of the men who have perished that day. Some stranger in Syracuse has died at the age of eighty-five, after a lifetime as the head of a manufacturing firm, and he muses, "This old geezer saw eighty-five. There's hope for me. It says he left a widow. Wonder if they had sex the night before he kicked off.

That is, if a man eighty-five can get an erection. Maybe that's what killed him."

He reads another obituary of a stranger, thinks, "This frenetic idiot died at forty-one. That's the advertising business for you. Why didn't I study architecture or some other serene profession, like archaeology?" As he finishes the last of the obituaries, the one-paragraph demises that line the bottom of the page, a triumphant thought shoots into his mind: "I'm glad it wasn't me."

He turns the page and reads about the latest murder trial, taking place in that winter sex spot of America, Miami. He avidly devours a description of incest, murder, illicit love, homosexuality, perverted sex, and exults, "That's living!"

By the time he has read the sports page and the stock market reports, which he has already painstakingly pored over the night before while going home on the train, he finds himself in Grand Central, disgorged into the cathedral-like station with thousands of other word-cannibal commuters. He doggedly strides the five blocks to his office building and in the elevator is pressed against the wall by a fat, moustached man. He thinks, "If that son-of-a-bitch plunges his elbow into my guts just once more, I'm going to swing at him." The man seems to read his thought and backs away.

At his floor, he walks out of the elevator down the corridor past the receptionist, thinking, "Does she or doesn't she?" as he stares at her hair, the combination of the colors of a tomato and a plum.

He steps into his office, which he has described to his wife as smaller than the death cell at Sing Sing. He rings for the twenty-two-year-old secretary he shares with the man in the next office, a newcomer to the firm, whom he scorns because he doesn't drink and doesn't play golf but seems hell-bent on dashing home each night to his bride of six months. "Six months!" he thinks disgustedly. "That's obscene. They probably have sex every night and all weekend. No wonder he hasn't time to learn golf."

The secretary teeters in on five-inch heels and black mesh stockings. He looks down from his six feet onto a crown of glossy black hair which curls in ringlets around a baby face thick with pancake makeup and inch-long false eyelashes that serve as visor to large, wistful blue eyes. He thinks, "What a dish. I wonder if she'd yell if I slipped my arm around those lovely curves? I didn't order that black leather couch just for the rear ends of my demented clients."

She daintily hands him a stack of mail, then totters out with a sad smile. He starts to rip open a letter but before he can read a word the buzzer on his desk summons him to the boss's office. He thinks, "That son-of-a-bitch is afraid I'll waste ten seconds of the precious time for which he's paying me the wages of a serf. Someday I'm going to saunter into his wood-paneled, brown-carpeted castle, smoking a cigarette—*not* one of our accounts— and puff the damned smoke right into his cancer-scared face. I'll say, 'You old goat, what do you mean telling me I should spend more time on the Smith account? I even slave over it weekends, giving up golf. The copy *is* good. I can't help it if you and Smith have the combined imagination of a water-soaked zombie.' "

Then, after "yes-sir-ing" his boss for twenty minutes, he returns to his professional cave to work through the day, with time out for a sandwich and coffee at his desk. He catches the train home, drinking three martinis on the way, staggers wearily into his split-level house and calls out, "Make me a martini, dear." He thinks, "Doesn't that mentally retarded woman I married know enough to have a martini ready? For twelve years, every single night I have to *ask* for a martini. She's quick enough to pour the Scotch for herself. I'll make it myself, like I always do. If I leave it to her, I'll get it just before the Late Late Show."

That night in their double bed, as he is about to turn off the light, he suddenly notices his wife is wearing a filmy blue nightgown which swirls gracefully around her knees. He thinks, "Pretty color. Like my secretary's eyes. Wonder how much it set me back? Ann *has* got a nice figure for an old married hag. Come to think of it, I haven't made love to her in two weeks. Maybe today's something special in our lives since she's all dolled up like Mrs. Astor's horse about to go to bed."

He turns and takes her in his arms. As he holds her close, he blots out the familiar face and shape of his wife. He pictures himself as a wealthy industrialist, say a Xerox executive vacationing in Majorca, making love to a lush blonde. The blonde looks exactly like Virna Lisi, whom he saw over the weekend in a funny movie with Jack Lemmon called *How to Murder Your Wife.*

And what about our average man's wife? What have been her fantasies during the day while he is off in the wilds of Urbania making a living by carving words for commercials that appear on their television screen, at which moments he pretends to throw up?

As she sits across from him at the breakfast table she thinks, "Why do I put myself through such torture? I could sleep until noon. I guess I feel the least a wife can do is to have coffee with her husband in the morning. My mother wouldn't do it, the fool. No wonder my father walked out on her. I don't intend to lose Jim that way. He's exposed to enough preying women who don't give a damn that he's somebody else's husband. Well, now that I'm up, I might as well get moving."

Her daughter, almost out the door, suddenly calls, "Hey, Mom, since you're on your feet, so to speak, how about a lift to school? My arches hurt from that Girl Scout hike to Hoboken."

"I'm not dressed, Barbara," she objects.

"Throw an old coat over that rag you're wearing. Who's going to look at *you,* anyhow?" Barbara goes to the hall closet, pulls out her mother's six-year-old lynx fur and hands it to her, wheedling, "Come on, Mums. I have a lot of books to carry today."

As though mesmerized, "Mums" walks out of the house and into the Chevrolet convertible. As she drives her daughter to school, she thinks, "Why do I let my fat little pixie coerce me like this? Can't I say no to her? If she walked more, she might knock off a pound or two.

Nobody drove me to school when I was her age. Not even in the damnedest downpour."

After depositing her daughter and a formidable stack of textbooks, as she drives home she thinks, "Jim only pecks me on the cheek every morning. When we were first married, he couldn't leave the house without kissing me like he was Clark Gable and I was Carole Lombard. Sometimes he even missed the 8:02 because he couldn't bear to leave without one more embrace. Now I'd drop dead if he ever suggested sex in the morning. We couldn't have it anyhow because Barbara is such a snoop she'd walk right into the room. Or scream like a stuck pig if we locked the door."

On reaching home, she bathes and dresses, thinks, "I'm going to take an hour and finish *The Collector.*" After shutting the book on the final page, she muses, "I wish a man would love me so much he'd want to chain *me* in his cellar so he could have me all to himself. Miranda was a nut to try to get away and cause her own death. And why did she rush him into sex so fast and then was disappointed when he couldn't perform? Maybe he was impotent. I imagine more young men are impotent than we know. Especially those who collect butterflies."

Slowly she pulls herself out of the fantasy world of fiction, markets over the telephone, tells Jennie, the cook, what to prepare for dinner, then drives to the local hospital where she serves as a volunteer three afternoons a week. She sits at the reception desk and tries to help new patients feel less worried by escorting them to their room, asking if there is anything she can do, reassuring relatives that everything will be fine.

Work over, she races down the steps of the hospital, collides against the sturdy chest of Dr. Malcolm Brown. He hugs her, asks, "When are we getting together again for bridge? I love to play with you, Ann. You're so good."

"I'll call Blanche tomorrow," she promises. As she skips away she thinks, "That dumb Blanche! Imagine that handsome, adorable, brilliant surgeon married to that empty-headed slut who redoubles without even a queen in her hand. If only *I* were his wife! I'd sure make him feel glad to come home at night, away from all the gore of that hospital. I'd be waiting at the door in tight, pink jersey stretch pants and a black velvet blouse cut down to my umbilical cord. And gold shoes with platform heels and golden earrings a mile long. And perfumed all over, and I mean *all* over, with Arpège. And holding out to him his favorite vodka and gin mixed. Such an exotic combination. Takes a man of real imagination to dream that one up. No dull, dry martini for him."

As she drives home she thinks, "When am I going to get the courage to fire Jennie? I can hardly be civil to her. She confuses all the telephone messages and she can't cook except for her twenty-seven-varieties fish stew, which Jim loathes. *Why* do I keep her after five years of culinary torture? Why? Because I'm chicken. She gets that sad look in her eyes, like a crippled horse about to be shot, and what can I do?"

When her husband walks in the door that evening and calls out, "Make me a martini, Ann," she replies sweetly, "In a minute, dear. I'm talking to Jenny about supper." She thinks, "That's all he ever asks for—drink and food. Bet he had five martinis on the train. I'll be damned if I'll contribute to his being an alcoholic. Let him make his own martini if he wants to dig his grave. And can't he at least ask how I am? He hasn't seen me all day."

She asks, "How did it go today, dear?" when she joins him in the study.

He answers, "Fine," sits down on the Paul McCobb couch and tears the wrapper off the latest copy of *Life*.

"Mr. Bigelow behaving?" she asks. She thinks, "No boss, not even a twentieth-century Simon Legree, could possibly be as brutal as Jim pictures Mr. Bigelow. Otherwise, he would have been murdered long ago by some enraged employee. Jim exaggerates. Just as he does, in reverse, about the number of drinks he had on the train. Tells me he only had one and reels in stinking like a gin factory."

"Fine," he says, deep in an article describing how Truman Capote spent six years in Kansas digging up the details of the murder of the Clutter family to fashion a best seller. He thinks, "The murdered family included a mother, father and two children." He looks up, asks, "Where's Barbara?"

"Upstairs studying," she says. She thinks, "I hope she's studying, not masturbating. That doctor who spoke to the PTA last week said eleven was a dangerous age for girls. He said their sexual feelings start to become aroused by members of the opposite sex, mostly their father, and they are likely to try to find a release in masturbating instead of repressing their feelings and using their libido—I think that's the word—for something constructive like studying Shakespeare. Wonder what I did with my aroused sexual feelings as a girl? My father was such a bastard I don't see how I could possibly have had one sexual feeling for him. Reeked all the time of cigars or those stinking fish he caught on weekends. But that doctor said even if a father looked like the monster in Frankenstein, a little girl would still adore him and want him for herself and want to kill off her mother. Hmm-mmmmm."

That night, getting ready for bed, she thinks, "I'll wear that new blue nightgown I bought on sale at Bonwit's last week. Five hundred to one, Jim won't even notice it."

Then, as her husband takes her in his arms, she thinks, "He must have had a good day at the office. Or read some sexy story riding home." And as he makes love to her, the vision of a man who looks like Dr. Malcolm Brown, who somewhat resembles Marcello Mastroianni, floats through her mind. She sees Jim as the blasé head of a harem whom she, as a young slave girl, rescues from a life of boredom and inspires to new heights of passion.

And their eleven-year-old daughter? What of the day-dream side of her life?

As her father stares at her across the breakfast table with what she senses is a harsh and critical eye, she thinks, "Hope he'll be in a better mood tonight so he'll let me go to the theater with Janet on Saturday. Mother's

afraid to decide because she knows he hates Janet's
mother because he thinks she's always drunk, even at
noon. But that doesn't mean he has to hate Janet, too.
I'm not like *my* mother, thank heavens."

She steals a look at her mother, thinks, "When I'm
married, if I *ever* turn up at breakfast looking like death
warmed over, I hope my husband shoots me. Why *hasn't*
Daddy shot her, I wonder? And the way she dresses me!
She'll put diapers on me next, just so *she'll* look younger.
She never lets me buy what the other kids are wearing.
She doesn't know what's *in*. She's an *out* person."

As her mother drops her at school, she kisses her
casually on the cheek as though she were a mentally
retarded friend who knew how to drive a car but not
much else. She hops out, lopes into the all-glass building.
She spends a good part of the next hour gazing dreamily
at a gangly dark-haired boy named Ben who sits in
front of her in geography class.

She thinks, "He sure is *dumb*, two years older than me
and in the same class, but he's *beautiful*. He'd look like
Ringo if his hair were a little longer. I guess I forgive him
for sticking that worm down my back at recess last week.
I *really* wouldn't have minded if he hadn't cut it up first.
I wonder if he plays with girls after school? I can just see
him in five years sailing away to India and bringing me
back emeralds and pearls and diamonds and rubies."

Her treasure-chest reverie is rudely interrupted by
Miss Lowry, the twenty-four-year-old teacher of geogra-
phy, who dares to demand, "Tell us where Saigon is,
Barbara."

"Vietnam," she says, pronouncing each syllable dis-
tinctly.

"What part of Vietnam?" snaps Miss Lowry.

"The south," says Barbara. She thinks, "What a
square! No wonder she's an old spinster. Thought she'd
trap me. Gave me a B last month because I tripped over
the spelling of Afghanistan. Why can't all teachers be
nice and sweet like Miss Scott? My father should have
married *her*."

The school day over, she visits for an hour with her friend Janet, then goes home and up to her room to study. The walls are lined with photograph after photograph of the Beatles in various poses—there are so many Beatle photographs that the green of the wall can be glimpsed only in a few, microscopic spots. One large poster, done by a commercially hep photographer, boasts *her* picture inserted in the center of the four beatifically grinning Beatles.

She opens her geography book and starts to memorize the chief cities of China. She thinks, "I should have stayed at Janet's a little longer. I could have heard 'She Loves Me' just *once* more. Why did Ringo get married? *And* have a baby? He's really much too young. He should have waited for me."

She sighs as she switches her gaze from a photograph of Ringo standing alone to the map of China. She thinks, "If I don't get an A in geography this month, Daddy won't *ever* let me see Janet. Then I'll run away from home like that girl did the other day, all the way to London just to see Ringo. Then Daddy won't ever see me again and won't he be sorry when he learns I have married an *astronaut,* maybe the first one on the moon, and I won't even invite Daddy to the wedding. It'll serve him right, the old square."

After dinner, after watching five television programs in a row on her own set, she kisses her parents goodnight as they sit reading in the study.

As she turns out the light and plops into bed, she thinks, "Poor Daddy and Mother. They never seem to get any fun out of life. He just works and reads or plays golf or watches TV if there's a football game on. They're both *always* so serious. I suppose that's because they're so *old.*"

In one minute flat she is off to the world of dreams and unconscious fantasies, getting fortified in sleep for another day of school and further encounters with the heroic Ben and the villainous Miss Lowry, the spidery spinster for whom she has, as yet, to devise the proper torture.

SOME PURPOSES OF FANTASY

Thus the average man, his wife, his children—all of us—are able to bear the rush, the routine, the eternal frustration of daily living because of one magnificent possession no one can take away—the ability to indulge in fantasy. Our capacity to dream while awake may save us at times from total chaos, from instant murder, from ignominious retreat and from suicidal despair.

As we grow up, most of us learn to accept three excruciating blows: to endure a certain amount of frustration when we wish something desperately and cannot get it, to acquire a sense of discipline and responsibility, and to give up certain pleasures of the body. In the first two or three years of life, we have to learn the inhibitions it took mankind a million or so years to develop.

Man is a creature of instinct just like the animal who instinctively mates, instinctively attacks when in danger, instinctively seeks food when hungry. But unlike the animal, man has a very complicated mind. This adds immeasurably to his satisfactions and pleasures. But it also may make life seem unbearable at times. Animals do not commit suicide out of inner despair.

Freud defined an instinct (or drive) as an internal stimulus of a bodily need such as hunger or thirst. He emphasized that an instinctual stimulus always acts as a continuing force, whereas an external stimulus may have only a single impact. He saw an instinct as possessing four elements: (1) its impetus or pressure (2) its aim, which is always satisfaction, the removal of the stimulus (3) its object, by means of which satisfaction is achieved (4) its physical source of stimulation.

Our instincts may propel us one way, but then the reasoning part of our mind may say "No!" So we behave in civilized fashion as far as our deeds go, even though we may be rebelling in thought and feeling.

But in fantasy, we may carry out the impulse in our mind. We can give some expression to a wish which, if acted upon, would have been dangerous to us. The greater evil would have been to act, not to fantasize.

In addition to being a psychic garment of safety, helping us survive and protecting us from engaging in destructive acts, fantasy also helps us maintain the image of ourselves as a noble, gallant, lovable human being, which, indeed, we are. Who in his right mind wants to see himself as selfish, greedy, envious, jealous, murderous, incestuous? Yet that we are, too.

For millions of years after man first appeared on earth, he appeared to have acted as though his impulse were all. Why the Ten Commandments? Because man realized he must set up rules to control his deepest, darkest desires. If you want to know what man considers his most dangerous wishes (from which most fantasies spring) read off the Ten Commandments. We are still fired by the same inner flames as the man Moses faced when he came down from the mountain. In addition to the Ten Commandments, we also now have laws that protect us from those who cannot control their urge to rape, murder, commit adultery or drink too much while driving. Fantasy helps most of us observe the laws by allowing us to break them in our imagination, if we need to do so. Thus we may think of fantasy, in one of its uses, as the psychic counterpart of a physical impulse that must be repressed.

One of the greatest uses of fantasy is to assuage our wounded pride. Lives there a man with psyche so dead who never to himself hath said, "Oh, if only I had thought of that comeback at the time!" The proper retort to a verbal attack often occurs after our assailant is out of harm's way. But we settle for second best as, in fantasy, we relive (and relieve) the moment of insult, devising an equal or even more devastating reply in return.

One woman, at a cocktail party, was introduced to a television star, the master of ceremonies of a children's program, who said to her enthusiastically, "You remind me of a movie star."

"Oh?" She beamed at what she thought would be a comparison to Brigitte Bardot.

"Yeah—May Robson," he snapped and sped off, leaving her speechless.

That night at home she said to her husband, "It took me until now to figure out the proper bon mot for that bastard. I should have replied sweetly, 'And you remind *me* of a movie star—Boris Karloff!'" It was at least some solace to her to imagine what she might have retorted.

A journalist who wrote a book about the life of a jockey was asked by the jockey, as the latter was about to appear on a television show, "Do you mind if I tell the audience that I wrote the book and you just did the editing?"

Hurt, but not knowing what to say, the writer mumbled his consent. Hours later, in the privacy of his home, he thought, "I should have said to him, 'Sure—go ahead and tell everybody you wrote every word of the book. But then be fair. Tell the audience I was the one who rode the horses!'"

Sometimes such a fantasy occurs in reverse. We think, "I wish I hadn't spoken so sharply—I could bite my tongue off," as we go over in our mind how we might have avoided a quarrel if only we had remembered that silence is golden. Or we think of the gifts we failed to send, the small but thoughtful acts we could have performed to brighten someone's life.

While much fantasy is sheer make-believe, fantasy can help dreams of glory come true. A boy may dream of being a great explorer and become one as a man. Or a bank clerk may have the fantasy he will be president of the bank and eventually be the president. Or a woman may dream of marrying a millionaire and be lucky enough to find a rich man she loves who falls in love with her. Freud called it the "realization of a daydream" when he received from America his first invitation to give a series of lectures on psychoanalysis and journeyed in 1909 to Clark University in Worcester, Massachusetts.

Fantasy forms the core of creativity. One man uses his fantasy to paint a work of art, another to design a skyscraper, a third to write a poem or compose a concerto.

The artist gives aesthetic form to his fantasies, using them in his and the world's behalf.

The scientist also may do this. Herman Kahn, in his book *Thinking About the Unthinkable,* tells how scientists consciously employ their fantasies to try to build a better world. The controlled fantasy of the actress as she uses her imagination to give depth to the portrayal of a role serves her in good stead. Businessmen take advantage of fantasy to build bigger and better industries. Athletes key themselves up for competition by going over in their minds how they intend to defend against possible attacks. Men and women embarking on important interviews use fantasy to visualize what questions may arise, how they will answer them, and thus feel more competent.

Sometimes fantasy itself may be the focus of a work of art, as in Elmer Rice's play *Dream Girl,* in which the heroine spends much of her life daydreaming, saying to herself, "If I could only stop lying awake for hours, dreaming up all the exciting things that could happen but never do."

A book in which fantasies comprise almost the entire story is *Alice in Wonderland.* What child, what adult does not revel in the artistry of the author, who, as Charles Lutwidge Dodgson, earned his living as a mathematician but who, as Lewis Carroll, was able to use his own fantasies to write an enchanting, enduring book about the fantasies of childhood.

A fantasy, at one and the same time, according to Freud, "hovers between three periods of time."[2] It is linked up with a current impression which has the power to rouse an intense desire. From there it "wanders back" to the memory of an early experience, generally belonging to infancy, in which the wish was fulfilled. Then it creates for itself a situation which is to emerge in the future, representing fulfillment of the wish. "So past, present and future are threaded, as it were, on the string of the wish that runs through them all."

"How many fantasies do I have?" one man demanded of his psychoanalyst.

"As many as you need," the analyst replied.

"I must have a million," the man muttered. "Sometimes I feel all is fantasy."

"Not quite," said the analyst. "Or you'd be in a mental hospital."

Today, we understand our emotions in the light of Freud's discoveries and the contributions of psychoanalysts who followed. We accept that there is a part of our mind of which we are only dimly aware, which often controls what we do and think. The more we are aware of this hidden part, the more we can control our acts consciously. It is in this hidden part that many of our fantasies whirl, causing us to act as we do, sometimes against our best interests.

Men and women who go into psychoanalysis to uncover the hidden part sometimes find it difficult at first to see any clear-cut division between their fantasy world and "reality." It all seems one world, miserable though that world may be. But slowly, to each one, comes the realization that he lives in two worlds. One is the world in which he must communicate with other people, the world in which he works and lives. The other is his secret world, in which exist wishes, fears and angers that even he does not know he possesses.

Everyone has fantasies, using them to escape reality, "to improve on reality," as Freud put it. Fantasies are part of us from the day we first try to make sense out of a world that frightens, frustrates, puzzles, pains and angers us, a world that at times seems full of non-sense.

Fantasy, in providing a temporary escape, helps us endure reality with more grace and dignity and humor than we might otherwise be able to muster. We need nobody, nothing, for we can use our imagination to dream what we will. In fantasy the poorest man in the world and the wealthiest are one.

No riches compare in psychological value with our ability to concoct the most exotic and erotic of love scenes, the wildest dreams of glory, the bloodiest of revenge. As Jean-Jacques Rousseau wrote, "The world of reality has its limits, the world of imagination is bound-less."

While many of our fantasies are, in essence, universal, each fantasy is unique to the one having it. It belongs in its embellishments to the person spinning it. No two people have exactly the same fantasy although the fantasy may reveal the same wish—a wish to be loved by Richard Burton or by Elizabeth Taylor, or the wish to write the Great American Novel or compose the Great American Symphony or select a stock that will triple in value in two months.

Fantasies are our one remaining, rightful claim to the childhood feeling of complete omnipotence, so hard for all of us to give up. The baby, in his first year of life, when he is helpless, is bound to feel he is boss of the world, that everyone else exists merely to carry out his commands. But he soon learns that to keep the love of his mother and father, who wish him to become a civilized little person, he must give up many of his own wishes and accept frustrations. To make acceptance of frustration easier, he resorts to fantasy. For childhood may be a chilling time.

Many of our conscious fantasies in adulthood are the disguised wishes and fantasies of childhood, Freud said. They are based on earlier editions of our own private fairy tales which have been repressed and emerge as the conscious fantasies of later life.

The man who sees himself, à la Walter Mitty, as the famous surgeon saving a life against incredible odds, or the great lover wooing thousands of women, is spinning a later version of the fantasy he had as a child of being a better man than his father and winning the love of the proud maiden, his mother. There is nothing wrong with this fantasy. Every son probably has it in one form or another, so that when he realizes he cannot have his mother, he is ready to seek another fair maiden and try to conquer the world for her, marry her and have children.

No one thinks it alarming when a little girl says seriously to her mother, "Please move out of the house so I can take care of Daddy" (not knowing, but having her own idea of what "taking care of" means). Or when a little boy tells his mother, "I want to marry you when I grow up. Let's get rid of Daddy." Or when a little boy looks unhappily at his new baby brother and says, "Let's send him back to the hospital. He doesn't belong here."

Little girls may have the fantasy their body was once like a little boy's, that they too possessed a penis, that mysterious, fascinating appendage of power and prestige. It is too humiliating to conceive of themselves as deprived of one, so they imagine they were born with a penis but that someone (usually their mother) took it away because they were "bad" (that is, masturbated or resisted toilet training).

To a boy, the fantasy may occur that he will lose his precious phallus if he is "bad" (masturbates or resists toilet training). For, upon seeing the naked body of a little girl, he may also conclude she had a penis once, like his, but lost it because she was "bad." Such evidence reinforces the fear that he may lose his too.

Who of a supposedly mature nature would dare to admit such wishes without fear of being thought freakish? Yet we all carry remnants of such childhood beliefs as part of our unconscious fantasy life. They may influence our behavior.

For instance, the man who is afraid of women sexually and who can accept only other men as sexual partners may be unconsciously in terror of the "penisless woman" who arouses his hidden fear of losing his own penis. The woman who has been unable to get married but is driven to compete with men in the world of work may be unconsciously trying to be a man, still possessing the fantasy that she once had a penis.

FANTASY AND REALITY

Our fantasy life is never "pure" fantasy but is based on what Freud called "a fragment of the truth." Put another way, according to Joan Riviere, a British psychoanalyst who has written about the nature of fantasy, "all phantasies are . . . *mixtures* of external and internal reality."

Fantasy is a "weapon which cuts both ways; it can be used to create goodness, and to destroy and expel badness," says Miss Riviere.[3]

Quoting Dr. Edward Glover, another British psychoanalyst, as emphasizing that even babies have a sense of reality of a kind, Miss Riviere says that from the very beginning of life the psyche responds to the reality of its experiences by interpreting them "or rather, *mis*interpreting them." The misinterpretation is due to the desire, natural in all of us, to avoid pain.

As children, because we cannot as yet use our full reasoning power, we are bound to make false assumptions and draw incongruous conclusions. We may believe, for instance, when we see our mother pregnant, that the new baby is caused by her eating too much food, or one particular food A three-year-old boy whose mother was carrying a baby snatched a piece of chocolate cake out of her hand, saying, "I don't want you to have another child." His fantasy was that eating chocolate cake (his favorite food) was responsible for the pregnancy.

As we grow up many different kinds of fantasies occur to us, woven around the experiences we go through—some of which may frighten us. But, if a child feels he has love, he will be able to handle his fantasies. They will not terrify or overwhelm him, either in childhood or in later life.

Miss Riviere speaks of love as "a complicated emotional attitude which has many stages and degrees in its development." She explains that love and understanding, patience and good judgment, can provide a stable world in which a child can feel that the bad or dangerous forces and impulses inside him will be withstood and controlled, and the good and helpful feelings and needs will be satisfied and encouraged. If he grows up in such an atmosphere, then "the storms of desire, hate and terror raging in him can vent themselves there without bringing him face to face with helplessness, despair and destruction."

We are in emotional distress only when fantasies become "over-luxuriant" and "over-powerful," in Freud's words. Like every other psychic mechanism we possess, fantasy, if used in moderation, enhances our life. But if its use becomes excessive, we may find ourselves in trouble.

For instance, some of us, at one time or another, may talk to ourselves in the privacy of our bedroom, or perhaps occasionally, while walking down the street, we will express a thought out loud. This is natural. But take the man or woman who marches along the sidewalk talking angrily to a ghost companion, not caring who hears (stand on any city street corner for ten minutes and you're likely to encounter such a person). Fantasy controls him, not he his fantasy.

Yet even the fantasy of talking to someone who isn't there can be made humorous and moving by an artist, as Mary Chase did in her play *Harvey*. The audience understood, as it laughed, why the slightly alcoholic hero had to create the ten-foot-tall rabbit, Harvey—out of his desperate loneliness and the feeling nobody loved him. Children talk to animals as though they were human beings to combat such loneliness.

What causes some people to abuse, instead of use, fantasy? The roots of all our fantasies are implanted in us during childhood. If someone's childhood has been very unhappy, he may retreat too far into the world of fantasy. The child *has* to resort to fantasy. He has little else to lessen the pain of a world he feels harsh and cruel.

In childhood all of us use fantasy to some degree to take care of the psychic wounds we experience as we face the ever-mounting evidence that our cherished omnipotence is a myth. We really *are* dependent upon the wishes and deeds of those tyrannical giants, our parents, who at first we believed to be our willing slaves. We must, at all costs, keep their love so they will continue to take care of us, feed us and make us feel as beloved as they can.

With most of us, the harshness of reality erodes our original narcissism so that we give up much of it, bit by bit, although never completely. We must retain some for what becomes confidence in and respect for ourselves.

But the person who cannot give up enough of his narcissism to live comfortably with himself or others has allowed his fantasies to become too destructive. They intrude to such an extent that they prevent him from concentrating on loving and working. Fantasies are dangerous when they replace action or productivity with constant daydreaming, if fantasy becomes what we call "delusion." The deluded person accepts his fantasy as reality. He has retreated too far into his dreams and wishes, lost in the orbit of his unconscious.

How deeply we live in the world of fantasy may determine the depth of depression. A depression may appear to stem from a vague feeling of despair and uneasiness but special fantasies underlie it.

What special fantasies are the cause of depression was one of the momentous discoveries made by Freud.

II

><><><><><><><><><><><><

Understanding
Depression

3

Depression, According to Freud

Depression thus has its roots in fantasy, both conscious and unconscious. The fantasies may spring from real or imagined hurts.

The real hurts, such as loss of a job, a violent argument with someone you love or cruel criticism of a creative effort, may temporarily shatter self-esteem. But if the depression lasts, then unconscious reasons are responsible. For the unconscious causes of depression are the truly powerful ones.

In reality, the death of a parent is one of the most devastating things that can happen and usually triggers a depression. We may experience feelings of guilt ("I could have been a better son [or daughter]."). We may wonder if there were more we could have done to keep our parent alive. We may think of the times we fought, the pain we may have caused and the pain the parent may have caused us.

We may in our grief draw closer to relatives, withdraw from all social contacts. The one who mourns is expected to take time to savor his sorrow. A year's grace is what society allows a mourner (during which time he is not supposed to remarry if he has lost a mate, or enjoy himself in any way). He is supposed to lose interest in work, to care about little except his loss. This is mourning, a time of external tears and "internal bleeding," in Freud's words.

Freud was well aware of the impact of the death of a

parent upon a child. He said that he reached his important discovery about the Oedipus complex after his father died. When Freud's mother died in 1930 at the age of ninety-five, Freud remarked, "I was not allowed to die as long as she was alive and now I may." He may have been referring to her great love for him which would have made his death a devastating blow, one he wanted to spare her, for he was his mother's favorite child.

When a parent dies, at first we are likely to feel a sense of unbelievable shock—it can't happen to us. Then follow the tears and sobs, and the body is left fatigued, drained by the psychic pain. For a while we move about in a world that does not seem real. Even the reality of death may be denied. We walk down the street and see someone who resembles the dead person and think, "There he is. He isn't dead after all!" Slips of the tongue referring to the dead person as though still alive may occur. We may say, "He's such a dear," when we meant to say, "He was such a dear."

Depression may also occur around the anniversary of the death of a parent. At certain times each year, we may feel depressed without knowing why. One man found that depression always struck the first week of every August, without understanding why. As he was speaking of this mysterious depression one day during his psychoanalytic session, he brought up the fact that his mother had died when he was a little boy.

"Do you remember the month?" asked the psychoanalyst.

"No," he said. "But I'll ask my father."

When he returned for his next session, he said in surprise, "My mother died when I was four years old on August the second. I had forgotten all about it."

"Your unconscious remembered," said the analyst.

Most sons and daughters go through a period of mourning for a dead parent, then resume life as it was before the death. But some never recover. A brilliant, beautiful woman, the wife of a Wall Street broker, had a reputation for great humor and cheerfulness until her mother died. Then she sank deeper and deeper into an unexplained depression and made several attempts to kill herself. Finally she succeeded, taking an overdose of sleeping pills. "Why? Why?" her friends asked each other in despair. On the surface she had everything— beauty, brains, a devoted, handsome, successful husband, three lavish homes, a married daughter, two grandchildren. But she had lost her mother and no longer wanted to live. Obviously, most of us do not react this drastically to a parent's death, although devastation is a part of mourning.

The most famous patient in psychoanalytic lore, Anna O., whose cure by Dr. Josef Breuer led Freud to the technique of free association, tried to kill herself after her father died. Breuer treated her by hypnosis during the months following her father's death and successfully helped her overcome her desire to commit suicide by allowing her to express her feelings.

The strong emotion that grips some after the death of a parent may not be caused by the loss alone. The feeling "my mother (or father) is dead and I want to die, too, because there is nothing more to live for" may hold more than pure mourning (as may other "obvious" causes of depression).

What this "more" is was revealed by Freud and elaborated upon over the years by psychoanalysts who studied the causes and cure of depression.

OF SEX REPRESSED

Freud discovered the cause of depression when he became interested in the difference between the "natural" mourning that occurs when someone you love dies and the "unnatural" melancholic feelings that are often part of depression. They may also be part of mourning for someone's death if the mourning lasts a long time or is intense and exaggerated.

Originally Freud linked depression to sex. He thought that repression of the sexual drive was the sole cause of depression. He later changed his view.

He first expressed his interest in depression in 1892 in

a letter to his friend Wilhelm Fliess, in which he included what he called Draft A, a description of "PROBLEMS," seven in all.[1] One of them was: "What is the aetiology [cause] of periodic depression?"

Underneath "PROBLEMS" he listed "Theses." His "thesis" on depression was that it constituted a form of "anxiety neurosis." At this early stage in his thinking, Freud believed that hysteria and anxiety neurosis, the two main categories of emotional illness at that time, were caused by sexual frustration in adulthood or sexual trauma in childhood, such as seduction by an adolescent or adult.

In a later Draft, sent to Fliess in June 1894, Freud wrote he had arrived at further conclusions about melancholia (as depression was then called when it was severe). He noted that often those who suffered from melancholia were "sexually anesthetic." They had no need for sexual intercourse or no sensations when they did indulge in it. Yet they had "a great longing for love in its psychical form."

Such persons were subject to "psychical erotic tension," which, if it accumulated and remained unsatisfied, resulted in melancholia, Freud held. Here we see the start of Freud's theory that fantasies caused depression, as he mentioned "psychical erotic tension," for the psyche is the birthplace and storehouse of fantasies.

He spoke in the letter of "gaps in his theory" which "sorely need filling." He himself was to fill in the gaps, one of them with his vital discovery of what he called "the great secret." This was the existence in the human mind of the countless fantasies which made up what Freud called "psychic reality," as compared to the objective reality of the world outside. Neurotics, he said, were guided by psychic reality rather than objective reality. The ruling factor in the psychology of the neurosis was the predominance of the life of fantasy and of the illusion born of an unfulfilled wish. The sense of guilt found in neurosis was "based upon the fact of an evil intention which was never carried out."

In other words, the fantasies in a mind could be so intense and compelling that they affected both psychic and physical well-being. If they became too powerful, insanity was the result.

Two months after this letter, on August 18, 1894, Freud sent Draft F to Fliess, with further observations about depression. He discussed the case of a twenty-seven-year-old man named Herr K., whose father had been treated for melancholia in his old age. Herr K. had been in good health until a short time before he saw Freud. He came for help after suffering short attacks of deep depression, lasting only a few minutes, which resembled complete apathy. He also had anxiety attacks when he felt his chest congested, and woke up at night trembling and feeling terrified.

In talking to Freud, the young man revealed that the year before, he had fallen in love with a girl who was quite a flirt, and it had been a shock when she told him she was engaged to someone else. But he claimed he no longer was in love with her.

He spoke frankly of his sexual activity. He told Freud that between the ages of thirteen, when he had been seduced at school, and seventeen, he had masturbated. After that, he was moderate in sexual intercourse, using a condom for fear of infection. He said he often felt "limp" after using it. He described the sexual act under this condition as "forced," and reported that his sexual desire had been greatly diminished during the past year. He had been very sexually excited by the girl who was a flirt; his first anxiety attack occurred the same evening after intercourse and his first night terror occurred two days after intercourse. Then, for three weeks, he was abstinent and felt peaceful, free from anxiety.

In discussing the case, Freud pointed out that the young man's father suffered from melancholia and, therefore, there might be a "disposition" to melancholia in the family. But, in addition, he said, there was a weakness in Herr K. when it came to the psychical mastery of bodily sexual excitement. This made it possible for anxiety to appear whenever there was an increase in his bodily excitement.

His feeling about the girl who aroused him sensually

caused a disturbance similar to the one found in the neurosis so common in men during long engagements, Freud said. But "above all," the young man's fear of infection and his decision to use a condom caused a conflict between his wish to enjoy sex and his fear of its consequences.

In short, said Freud, the young man brought "psychical sexual enfeeblement" on himself because he took a dislike to intercourse. Yet, because his physical health and his production of sexual stimuli were unimpaired, the situation led to anxiety. Freud added that the young man's readiness to take precautions, instead of finding adequate satisfaction in a safe sexual relationship, "pointed to a sexuality which was from the start of no great strength."

Then Freud discussed the case of a forty-four-year-old man who became depressed after intercourse with his wife. Freud said it was quite possible that the starting point of a minor melancholia may be an act of intercourse, "an exaggeration of the physiological dictum: *omne animal post coitum triste* [every animal is sad after intercourse]." This man also used a condom, which Freud called evidence of weak potency and added, "being something analogous to masturbation, it acts as a continuous causative factor of his melancholia."

In a letter written six months later, on January 7, 1895, Freud drew a connection between depression and masturbation. He said that depression could arise as an intensification of neurosis because of masturbation. (Many of his depressed patients in their analyses spoke of frequent masturbation.)

In this letter Freud stated at length what he thought was the cause of melancholia. He described the emotion corresponding to melancholia as "mourning or grief, that is, longing for something that is lost." He added that in melancholia there was probably a question of loss in the person's instinctual life.

He noted that many young girls suffered a nervousness that seemed to him to be melancholia, occurring when their sexuality was undeveloped. Such a girl, he said, often asserts that she has not eaten "simply because she has no appetite and for no other reason. Loss of appetite—in sexual terms, loss of libido." (Dr. Karl Abraham was later to say of depressed persons who overate that "food has taken the place of love.")

Freud concluded, "So it would not be far wrong to start from the idea that *melancholia consists in mourning over loss of libido*" (italics his).

(Elsewhere, Freud defined "libido" as the energy, "regarded as a quantitative magnitude, though not at present actually mensurable," of those instincts which have to do with all that may be comprised under the word "love." He included not only the love that poets sing of, sexual love with sexual union as its goal, but the love of self, love for parents and children, love for friends, humanity in general, concrete objects and abstract ideas. Psychoanalytic research, he said, revealed that all these tendencies to love were an expression of the same instinctive activities. In relations between the sexes, these instincts forced their way toward sexual union, but in other circumstances they were diverted from this goal or prevented from reaching it, though always keeping enough of their original nature to preserve a recognizable identity.)

Freud noted "striking connections" between melancholia and sexual anesthesia. He asked rhetorically why sexual anesthesia played a part in melancholia (referring to the observation that depressed men and women often appeared uninterested in sex). He said that a melancholic person usually had had difficulty all his life becoming sexually aroused.

Freud also raised the question why sexual anesthesia (or frigidity) seemed so predominantly a characteristic of women. He answered it by saying he thought this stemmed from the passive part played by women. Women become sexually anesthetic more easily than men because their entire upbringing aims not at arousing sexual feelings in the body but at translating into psychic stimuli (fantasies) any excitement which might otherwise arouse them physically, he said.

In other words, instead of expressing their sexual feelings in immediate action, women have to adopt seductive measures "calculated to entice men to perform the specific action," as Freud put it. Then, because they run the risk of a man not following through sexually, they are likely to keep their physical sexual desire at a low key so they do not feel too frustrated should this happen.

Freud spoke of both physical and psychological factors in sexual arousal. He believed at this time that the physical energy for sex was stored in what he called "the terminal organ," located somewhere in the body near the genitals. The psychic energy for sex was related to fantasies in the mind, often associated with the memory of previous sexual experiences.

Freud held that a low level of tension in the terminal organ seemed to constitute the main disposition to melancholia. Where this low level was present, any neurosis easily took on "a melancholic stamp." He added that whereas "potent" individuals easily acquired anxiety neuroses, "impotent" ones inclined to melancholia.

He then asked how the effects of melancholia could be explained. He described these effects as "psychical inhibition accompanied by instinctual impoverishment, and pain that this should be so."

It was here that Freud expanded his theory of melancholia to include more than a reaction to repressed sexuality. In terms of what happened to the body, he said that when the psychical sexual group (the fantasies in the mind) suffered very great loss in the amount of excitation (excitement), this might lead to a kind of *"indrawing in the psyche"* (italics his). This produced an effect of suction upon the adjoining amounts of excitation. The neurones associated (with the fantasies) were obliged to give up their excitation, and this produced pain, for the "uncoupling of associations" was always painful, he held.

Then there set in an impoverishment of excitation—of reserve stock—in a way that resembled *"internal bleeding"* (italics his). This showed itself in the other instincts and functions. This indrawing process had an inhibiting effect and operated like a wound, in a manner analogous to the theory of physical pain.

The counterpart to this could be seen in mania (over-elation), where an overflow of excitation is communicated to all the associated neurones, Freud maintained. Here there was a similarity to neurasthenia, where a very similar impoverishment arose owing to the excitation running out, "as it were, through a hole." In neurasthenia, what was pumped empty was sexual excitation in the body, while in melancholia, "the hole is in the psyche." But neurasthenic impoverishment could extend to the psyche, and sometimes the manifestations of these two conditions were so similar they could only be differentiated with difficulty.

Two years later, on May 31, 1897, Freud sent Fliess his Draft N, headed "NOTES (III)," which set forth the theory that proved the foundation of all future discussion of depression. This draft contained the core of his later classic paper "Mourning and Melancholia."

He declared that hostile impulses against parents (a wish that they should die) are an integral part of neuroses. These wishes come to light consciously in the form of obsessional ideas. In paranoia, for instance, delusions of persecution, the supposed murderous threats by unseen and unknown enemies stem from the wish to kill projected on others.

The impulse to kill a parent is repressed at times when pity for the parent is paramount, such as when he falls ill or dies. If a parent dies, one of the manifestations of grief is to reproach the self for the parent's death, to become melancholic, Freud said. Or to punish the self in a hysterical way, by putting the self in the place of the dead parent as retribution.

Freud held that it seems as though in sons the death wish is directed against the father, in daughters, against the mother. He illustrated this theory by the example of a servant girl who transfers her original wish to kill her mother to a wish that the mistress for whom she works were dead so she could marry the master of the house.

The last mention of depression in a letter to Fliess

appeared on January 16, 1899. Freud wrote that a patient of his was continually plunged into despair by the gloomy conviction that she was useless and good for nothing. He commented, "I always thought that in early childhood she must have seen her mother in a similar state, in an attack of real melancholia." It is interesting that as early as 1899 Freud spoke of a mother's depression having an effect on a child, a theory later studied and elaborated upon by a number of psychoanalysts, including his own daughter, Anna.

"MOURNING AND MELANCHOLIA"

In his historic paper "Mourning and Melancholia," written in 1915 and published in 1917, Freud revised and clarified his original theories.[2] By comparing melancholia and the normal emotion of grief as expressed in mourning, he hoped to throw some light on the nature of melancholia, he said.

He described mourning as the reaction to the loss of a loved person. Or the loss of some abstraction which has taken the place of the loved one, such as an ideal, or the fatherland, or liberty. But in some, instead of a state of grief, melancholia developed. Although grief involved "grave departures" from a normal attitude to life, it was not regarded, as melancholia was, as a pathological condition for which psychological treatment was urged, he said.

Freud spoke of the distinguishing mental features of melancholia as:

> . . . a profoundly painful dejection, abrogation [abolishing] of interest in the outside world, loss of the capacity to love, inhibition of all activity, and a lowering of the self-regarding feelings to a degree that finds utterance in self-reproaches and self-revilings, and culminates in a delusional expectation of punishment.

With one exception, the same reactions appear in grief, he said. The exception is the lowering of self-esteem. "In grief, the world becomes poor and empty; in melancholia it is the ego itself [which becomes poor and empty]."

Freud saw the psychic purpose of mourning as the testing of a reality in which the loved one no longer existed. The libido had to be withdrawn from its attachment to the loved one. Bit by bit, at great expense of time and energy, memories and hopes were relinquished, usually painfully. But when the work of mourning was finished, the ego had once again become free and uninhibited and the libido could be turned to some other love.

In other words, upon the death of someone you love, it is normal to mourn for a period of time. But if this mourning lasts for years it is melancholia, or depression.

Melancholia can also be the reaction to the loss of some loved one who has not died, Freud observed. He cited the example of a bride left at the altar. In other instances, a depressed person may experience the feeling of loss and yet not know exactly what it is he has lost. In still others, the person knows whom he has lost but not what in them he has lost. This would suggest, Freud stated, that melancholia was in some way related to an unconscious loss of someone you love, as differentiated from mourning. In the latter, you are conscious of whom or what you have lost.

Just as in mourning, the unknown loss in melancholia results in "an inner labor," which leads to inhibition. But the inhibition of the melancholiac seems puzzling, Freud said, because we cannot see what it is that absorbs him so completely.

Referring to the accusation of the self which takes place in the melancholiac but not in the mourner, Freud stated, "He [the melancholiac] must surely be right in some way and be describing something that corresponds to what he thinks. . . . He really is as lacking in interest, as incapable of love and of any achievement as he says."

The essential thing is not whether the melancholiac's "distressing self-abasement" is justified in the opinion of others but that in his own lamentations he is correctly describing how he feels. He has lost his self-respect and he must have some good reason for this loss. If he suffered in the same way as one who lost a parent through death, he would be mourning the dead person. But according to what the melancholiac says, the loss lies within himself.

Freud clinically described what took place. One part of the ego of the melancholiac sets itself against a second part and judges it critically, as if it were another person. The part that sits in judgment is the super-ego, or conscience.

"In the clinical picture of melancholia, dissatisfaction with the self on moral grounds is far the most outstanding feature," Freud observed.

Continuing this line of thought, which led to his new theory of depression, Freud noted that if you listen patiently to the many and various self-accusations of the depressed person, you cannot avoid the impression that often the most violent of the accusations are not applicable to him. They fit someone else, some person "whom he loves, has loved or ought to love." Freud adds, "So we get the key to the clinical picture—by perceiving that the self-reproaches are reproaches against a loved object which has been shifted on to the patient's own ego."

In other words, everything derogatory the depressed person says about himself applies to someone else. This explains why he really does not hang his head in shame and show an attitude of humility and submission as would befit his supposed worthlessness. Instead, he causes a great deal of trouble, draws attention to himself all the time, perpetually takes offense, and behaves as if he were treated with great injustice, Freud stated.

All this is possible only because the reactions expressed . . . proceed from an attitude of revolt, a mental constellation which by a certain process has become transformed into melancholic contrition.

Why the contrition? Here Freud explained the heart of his theory. The libido, which in mourning ordinarily is freed after a year or so and directed to someone else, in melancholia serves only to establish an "identification" with the abandoned loved one, who is not really given up.

Freud defined "identification," a very important concept in the theory of depression, in a paper on "Group Psychology and the Analysis of the Ego," written in 1921. He explained it was "the earliest expression of an emotional tie with another person."[3] One way we learn, as babies, is through identifying with our parents, consciously and unconsciously adopting their attitudes, copying their behavior.

In later life, if there has been too intense an identification with a parent, it may keep us from seeing ourselves or others very clearly. Identification may also be a way of trying to keep within us someone we love who has been lost to us. Freud gives the example of a child who, unhappy over the death of a kitten, announced he was the kitten and crawled about on all fours.

We identify, as children, with our parents through a mental mechanism called "introjection." We might think of this process as a psychic swallowing of someone we love. One instance of introjection of the loved one is provided by the analysis of melancholia, said Freud. He referred to melancholia as a state of mind which "counted among the most remarkable of its causes the real or emotional loss of a loved object."

Referring to the melancholiac's cruel self-depreciation of the ego, combined with relentless self-criticism and bitter self-reproaches, Freud said that this disparagement and these reproaches applied at bottom to the loved one and "represent the ego's revenge upon it."

Persons who are depressed "show us the ego divided, fallen into two pieces, one of which rages against the second," he said. "This second piece is the one which has been altered by introjection and which contains the lost object."

In "Mourning and Melancholia" Freud described once again the erotic life of man. During the first phase, which usually comes to an end by the time we are five years old, we have found the first object for our love in one or other of our parents. All our sexual instincts, with their demand for satisfaction, have been united upon this parent. Then repression sets in (due to the taboo against incest). This compels us to renounce the greater number of our infantile sexual aims and causes "a profound modification" in our relationship to our parents. We still remain tied to them but our sexual instincts become "inhibited in their aim." The love which we henceforth feel toward them is no longer incestuous and rivalrous but tender. Our earlier sensual tendencies, however, remain more or less strongly preserved in the unconscious part of the mind, so that the whole of the original current continues to exist, underground.

At puberty, new and very strong conscious tendencies with directly sexual aims arise. In what Freud called "unfavorable cases," the tendencies remain separate; the sensual current and the "tender" emotional trends are split, rather than combined. Such a man will show a sentimental enthusiasm for women whom he deeply respects but who do not excite him, and will be sexually attracted only to women whom he does not love, perhaps thinks little of or even despises.

Usually, however, the adolescent succeeds in bringing about a degree of synthesis "between the unsensual, heavenly love" and the "sensual, earthly love," according to Freud. His relationship with his sexual object contains both the uninhibited instincts and those inhibited in their aim (the tender ones). The depth to which anyone is in love, as contrasted with his purely sensual desire, may be measured by the size of the share taken by the inhibited instincts of tenderness, Freud maintained.

The fact that the loved one enjoys a certain amount of freedom from criticism, and all his characteristics are valued more highly than those of someone not loved, Freud described as the phenomenon of sexual overestimation. The tendency which thus falsifies judgment is that of "idealization." The ego becomes more and more unassuming and modest, and the object more and more "sublime and precious," until at last the object gets possession of the entire self-love of the ego, whose self-sacrifice follows as a natural consequence.

In "Mourning and Melancholia" Freud further explains melancholia as the reaction to a real loss of a loved object but over and above this "bound to a condition which is absent in normal grief or which, if it supervenes, transforms normal grief into a pathological variety."

This condition comes about because of the conflict inherent in ambivalence (mixed feelings of love and hate). The ambivalence "casts a pathological shade on the grief, forcing it to express itself in the form of self-reproaches, to the effect that the mourner himself is to blame for the loss of the loved one, i.e., desired it."

Freud pointed out that the person incapable of mature love, who can love only in a childish, narcissistic, selfish way, is apt to regress to the primitive stages of his psychosexual development when threatened by the loss of someone he loves. The three main stages of this psychosexual development are the oral (when pleasures of sucking and biting dominate the baby's world), the anal (when he gains control over his anal sphincter and can decide either to please his mother with compliance or spite her) and the genital (when interest moves to this organ and Oedipal desire enters the picture).

And, said Freud, it is primarily the sadistic aspect of the oral stage (biting) and of the anal stage (spite and anger) with which one combats a loss. It is this sadism alone which "solves the riddle of the tendency to suicide which makes melancholia so interesting and so dangerous."

He then went straight to the heart of depression. "We have long known it is true that no neurotic harbors thoughts of suicide which he has not turned back upon himself from murderous impulses against others, but we have never been able to explain what interplay of forces can carry a purpose through to execution."

The analysis of melancholia, he explained, now showed that the ego can kill itself only if, owing to the power of the loved one as retained within as image, it can treat itself as the loved one, directing against itself all the rage it feels for the other person. In Freud's words, "the shadow of the object," the loved one, falls upon the ego so that part of the latter can be criticized as though it were the forsaken object.

Freud pointed out that in the two opposed situations of being intensely in love and of suicide, the ego is overwhelmed by the loved one, although in totally different ways. (He once commented, "One is very crazy when one is in love.")

Freud spoke of his theory that suicide is unconscious murder in "The Psychogenesis of a Case of Female Homosexuality," written in 1914. He maintained in this paper that no one could find the psychical energy to kill himself unless he were also unconsciously killing someone with whom he identified.

In other words, ". . . each man kills the thing he loves," but only if he is depressed and full of unconscious hate. The depressed person kills the thing he loves-hates, the thing over which he feels guilty because of his hate. This hate overrides his love, which is not mature love but the possessive, demanding, hungry love of a child.

DEPRESSION: THE WISH TO KILL TURNED ON THE SELF

As much as he hates himself, thus, the depressed person hates the one he believes has hurt him. The degree of hate is related to the degree of identification with that other person, explains Dr. Walter A. Stewart.[4]

This identification is the key to the understanding of deep depression and suicide, he points out. Caught in the conflict between love and hate, the depressed person has difficulty distinguishing between the self and the one he loves-hates. Hating the other person and hating himself is one and the same thing.

"It is when you hate the other person and are merged with him, that you can kill yourself, which is indistinguishable from killing the other person," says Dr. Stewart. "This was Freud's discovery and is the essential point in the understanding of the psychiatric depression and the suicide which may accompany it."

Because there is love as well as hate, the *conflict* between the love and the hate causes the depression. The main purpose of depression, according to Dr. Stewart, is to handle aggression in a regressive way by turning the aggression back on the self because there *is* love—otherwise the hate would triumph and the person would commit murder.

The psychotic depression (the very deep depression) differs from the neurotic one, says Dr. Stewart, in that the former is based on intense self-hatred. The neurotic may feel, "I don't think I'm lovable, I am not living up to my expectations, I feel blue, low." But the psychotic actively hates himself and his depression is far more intense. Inability to love the self is different from actively hating the self, Dr. Stewart adds.

In the case of suicide, the hate overpowers the love, so much so that the self and object are no longer differentiated.

The person hates himself and the object, the two go hand in hand, so that the wish to murder is fully gratified when he commits suicide. It is as if he killed the other person as he kills himself. It doesn't really matter which one he kills. In his unconscious it is death to both.

Any act as extreme as suicide has its roots in infancy and pertains to the relationship between mother and child. The suicide is killing his "bad" mother. The baby who feels unloved will believe his mother "bad" but needing her desperately will turn this around and say, "I am bad, she is good." The more frustrating the mother, the less love she gives, the less she knows what her baby needs and wants, the "badder" she is to him. This badness he then takes unto himself, and the hatred within may simmer over the years. In essence, every murder is the unconscious murder of the "bad" mother, as is every suicide.

The depressed person, who has incorporated the "bad" mother, "punishes the lost object in effigy" when he commits suicide, Dr. Stewart puts it. He adds, "But his own ego becomes the effigy which he punishes, as Dr. Bertram Lewin has pointed out."

One of the goals of depression is to get rid of the "badness" in both the self and loved-hated one in order to regain the mutual love that supposedly existed at first. Suicide is the last-ditch attempt to do so.

Suicides often have a fantasy of revenge just before they kill themselves. They think, "He (or she) will feel guilty because I am dead." Thus they express the wish to ruin with guilt and remorse the life of the one who has so deeply hurt and disappointed them.

Fury is often shown in notes left by those who commit suicide or attempt to. They speak of a desire for vengeance and the hope that their death "will haunt" the person to whom the note is addressed. Harry Milt, psychologist and writer,[5] tells of a young man who tried to kill himself with an overdose of pills after being fired. He left a note on his desk reviling his supervisor, saying, "I am going to die and I will make you pay for this." The note was found in time, the police rushed to the rooming house where he lived and saved his life. In another instance, a wife told her husband, who wanted a divorce, "I will kill myself and it will be on your head." She made several attempts, none successful. But other wives have succeeded after making the same threat.

Thus, according to psychoanalytic theory no one commits suicide unless at the same time he unconsciously is killing another person to whom he is deeply attached yet whom he hates. He turns on himself a death wish directed against the other person. This is how Freud explained what he called "the enigma of suicide."

It may seem paradoxical that the act of killing oneself symbolizes the murder of another. But, as Freud explained, the one who is both loved and hated has been psychically taken inside as a way of holding on to him, and has become a permanent part of the self. A child whose mother leaves him alone a good deal of the time and who is anguished by the frequent separations, psychically "incorporates" her so he still possesses her in fantasy. (What psychoanalysts call "oral incorporation" represents the most primitive form of ambivalent relationship, in that it is experienced as a method both of destroying and preserving the object.) The child also will hate his mother for deserting him, because he feels a deep need for her. He wishes her dead, both the actual mother and the image of her now locked within him.

So when a suicide kills himself he is in fantasy also killing the person who has psychically become a part of him. The fact that he is also killing himself does not register in his unconscious because there is no concept of death of the self in the unconscious. (We never die in a dream but always wake before our death occurs, if it threatens.) The self lives on forever, as far as our unconscious, which believes in magic, is concerned.

If Freud's theory of suicide is applied in lesser degree to depression, the latter is seen to stem from the wish to kill someone toward whom we hold deep feelings of mixed love and hate. We believe we want to kill him because in the unconscious, hatred automatically carries with it the fantasy that the loved one must die. There is another fantasy in the unconscious which also haunts us—that the wish is the same as the deed, and therefore we must punish ourselves for our imagined guilt.

Depression thus is a turning inward of murderous wishes not intense enough to drive to suicide but intense enough to make for torment. Depression, in a way, is death to the self administered in small psychic doses.

4

Added Illumination:
Abraham's Theory of Depression

Freud started the move to understand depression as related to the whole of a life, not merely to the specific tragedy that triggered it.

After his first allusions to depression in the letters to Fliess, Freud wrote little about it until 1915, when "Mourning and Melancholia" appeared. But four years before this, Dr. Karl Abraham, one of Freud's close friends and most brilliant colleagues, wrote a paper in which he discussed his own theory of depression.[1]

Abraham was a pioneer in the study of depression, especially manic-depressive insanity, an illness marked by fluctuations between extreme elation (mania) and deepest melancholia.

He traced adult depression back to what he called the "primal depression of infancy." He theorized that if one became depressed as an adult, he had first gone through a primal depression.

This depression, according to Abraham, preceded and set the pattern for adult depression. The latter, "in the last resort . . . is derived from disagreeable experiences in the childhood of the patient."

He related melancholia to retreat from a severely disturbing situation to an early infantile pleasurable period. In other words, when reality becomes too difficult, we will regress to the level of behavior appropriate to an

70

earlier time in life when we did not have to struggle so hard, when pleasure came more easily.

He saw the despair of a psychotic person as the result of a loss, the renunciation of a sexual goal or a loved person.

RAGE AT EVERY PSYCHIC STAGE

Abraham stressed the importance of the conflict of ambivalence in depression. Feelings of love and hate in the depressed person seemed almost equal as they pulled against each other and the result was paralysis of feeling, he said.

In all of us, part of becoming mature is the ability to face and handle our mixed feelings of love and hate. When we can cope with our buried hatred (and we all possess such hatred), we can then take the energy formerly used to keep the hatred repressed and let it flow into love and work.

During a personal psychoanalysis, both the love and hate for a parent must be faced and accepted, for depression to be overcome. One woman mourned her father's death for ten years, until, on the couch, she was able to acknowledge her great hatred for him, denied through the years. She hated him in part because of his behavior when she was a child, including physical violence at times and, when she was ten, walking out on his family to marry another woman. Until the analysis she had always adored him, thought he could do no wrong and never blamed him for abandoning what she thought of as her unattractive mother.

Another woman, whose mother had died when she was three, lived with depression for twenty-five years. While in analysis, she discovered a hidden unconscious wrath at her mother for dying. As a small child she thought her mother had willfully deserted her, leaving her in the clutches of a selfish, cruel stepmother. This fantasy had persisted in her unconscious until uncovered during treatment. She came to see she had viewed her mother's death through the eyes of an abandoned, emotionally troubled child.

In his paper on depression, Abraham stated that the hatred in melancholia, first felt during the primal depression, is directed chiefly against the mother. The small child holds destructive wishes towards the mother who frustrates him, as she is bound to do. Yet he also wants to save her from destruction, since if she disappears from the earth, who is left to feed, care and comfort him? As Dr. Walter A. Stewart says, "You can't eat your mother and have her, too." So the baby turns his rage inward and becomes depressed.

We show rage at every psychic stage. Our earliest anger is known as oral hostility or oral aggression, since it occurs at the time of life when our mouth is the most important organ. With it we explore the world—we use it for the pleasure it gives in sucking and biting, and to coo and scream out of. This explains why so many depressed persons take to drink, the swallowing of pills and extreme attitudes toward food, either refusing it or stuffing themselves out of a fear of starving. We never completely leave behind the wishes of the oral stage. It is only when they become so intense that they dominate us that we are said to have regressed to that stage.

Drinking, eating, the swallowing of pills—in addition to containing oral aggression these acts embody a certain amount of oral eroticism, which is also present in depression, Abraham observed. Strong oral rage is likely to be accompanied by strong oral eroticism, for at this early stage in life our two main drives, sexual and aggressive, are closely intertwined.

Abraham declared that "every state of depression, just like every anxiety-state, to which it is closely related, contains a tendency to deny life." In those days a distinction was made between the diagnosis of depression and of an anxiety state; today most psychoanalysts find that where there is one, there is usually the other.

WHEN YOU CAN'T LOVE, YOU HATE

In a person suffering from "neurotic depression," according to Abraham, the libido does not develop in a normal way because the two opposing tendencies, love and hate, interfere with each other. The depressed person is inclined to adopt a hostile attitude toward the world, a hostility so great that his capacity for love is reduced to a minimum. "At the same time he is weakened and deprived of his energy through the repression of his hatred or, to be more correct, through repression of the originally overstrong sadistic component of his libido."

Abraham described a depressed person as one whose "libido has disappeared from the world, as it were."

The depressed person's inability to establish his love and interest in a definite way causes him to have a general feeling of uncertainty which leads to excessive doubting. In this state, he "is neither able to form a resolution nor to make a clear judgment; in every situation he suffers from feelings of inadequacy and stands helpless before the problems of life."

Abraham cites one of his patients, who, shortly after becoming engaged, was overcome by a feeling of incapacity to love and fell into a severe melancholic depression. This happened with several patients and in each instance unconscious hate was found to be paralyzing the capacity to love.

The depressed person feels he is hated and believes himself inferior and defective, according to Abraham. In return, he hates, but represses it. He seethes with a violent desire for revenge, which he does not put into action. He ascribes his feelings instead to "the torturing consciousness" of his own defects, instead of to his "imperfectly repressed sadism."

Every depressed person, according to Abraham, tends to draw the same conclusion as Shakespeare's Richard III, who lists all his failings with pitiless self-cruelty and then sums up:

*"And therefore, since I cannot prove a lover . . .
I am determined to prove a villain."*

Put another way, in Abraham's view depression is a
result of instinctual drives paralyzed by conflict. Guilt
follows the suppression of frequent impulses of hatred
and revenge. The more violent the unconscious impulses
of revenge, the more marked the tendecy to form fantasies of guilt, and the deeper the depression.

In depressed persons, what Abraham called "an insatiable sadism" directed toward all persons and all things
has been repressed into the unconscious and guilt results.
Nevertheless, he added, the very idea of guilt contained
the fulfillment of a wish—the repressed wish to be "a
criminal of the deepest dye, to have incurred more guilt
than everyone else put together."

As a result of the repression of sadism, there arises
depression, anxiety and self-reproach, and also reinforcement of the masochistic tendency, which is guilt, Abraham explained.

There is also pleasure in depression, he held. A
depressed person gets pleasure from his suffering and from
continually thinking about himself. "Thus, even the
deepest melancholic distress contains a hidden source of
pleasure." When the pleasure changed to pain, a person
would do something about his depression, he said (either
pull himself out of it, or kill himself, or seek a psychoanalyst).

In seeing depression as a regression to earlier psychosexual stages, Abraham recognized, as did Freud, that the
depression of infants was a precursor of all later depression. He also related drug addiction to depression. He
declared that the addict clings to his drugs with the same
despair shown by the depressed person clinging to his
image of the lost loved one.

In a letter to Freud on March 31, 1915, Abraham
listed the basic points of Freud's theory as: the depressed
person has lost something but does not know what, the
ego is impoverished, the depressed person identifies with
the object of his love, and his narcissistic identification

prevents him from putting his energy into loving someone else.[2]

To this, Abraham stated that he would emphasize the sadistic aspects in depression. He evidently felt Freud did not stress enough the sadism in depression, a sadism from the oral stage, which arose out of the very early depression caused by a child feeling unloved by his mother and then becoming furious at her.

5

<hr>

Further Contributions: Klein, Spitz, Bowlby, Mahler and Others

Following Freud and Abraham, a number of psychoanalysts started to study the depression of the early years of life as it related to later depression.

KLEIN: THE DEPRESSIVE POSITION

A woman now came to the forefront, Melanie Klein. She contributed the theory of a "depressive position," which, she maintained, occurred in the life of every infant.

Freud and Abraham both met Mrs. Klein for the first time at the Psychoanalytic Congress held in The Hague in 1920. Abraham was so impressed with her work that he invited her to practice in Berlin, where he had started a psychoanalytical institute. The following year she moved to Berlin from Budapest, where she had settled with her husband and three children.

Mrs. Klein was one of those who extended psychoanalytic understanding into the very early stages of infancy. She treated her first child, a five-year-old boy, in 1919, and after this came others, including a two-year-old girl. Mrs. Klein found that in play the child used toys to express symbolically his fantasies and anxieties. By interpreting both the child's words and his play, she applied the basic principle of free association to treatment.

During her analysis of children, she became impressed

with the power, and what might often be the terror, of fantasy.[1] She described fantasy as "the psychic representative of instinct." She held, "There is no impulse, no instinctual urge or response which is not experienced as unconscious phantasy . . . A phantasy represents the particular content of the urges or feelings dominating the mind at the moment."

Mrs. Klein gave psychoanalysis the phrase "depressive position," after studying children and concluding there were two "positions" which occurred in the first year of life. She used the term "position" rather than "stage of development" to emphasize the coexistence of feelings in the earlier stage with those of the later one, rather than a complete move out of a first stage into a second.

The first position, occurring in the first six months of life, she called the "paranoid-schizoid" position. The second she named the "depressive" position. They were both part of a normal development, according to her.

The first position occurs when an infant, frustrated in getting what he wants, whether milk, a change of diapers or a warm blanket to protect him from the cold, imagines his mother is deliberately persecuting him. At this stage of life he does not possess enough reason to figure out that his mother may be delayed by household chores, or too fatigued to stir for the moment. He believes she, and the world, exist only to fulfill his needs. If the mother fails to carry out his slightest wish, he becomes furious at her. He imagines she is persecuting him and he hates her. (Later paranoid delusions may be caused by these very early experiences. A man's belief that he is being poisoned may go back to his fantasy as a baby that his mother was trying to poison him. If a mother, for instance, strongly resents having a baby, her anger may be communicated to the baby at her breast. She may feed him as though she hated to do so and he may feel "poisoned," not by the milk itself [obviously if the milk were poison he would have been dead long ago] but by her hate, as food and hate become forever inseparable in his mind.)

After the paranoid position occurs the second or depressive position. As the infant begins to take in more of the world about him and starts to develop a conscience, he feels guilty because of his anger at what he believes to be his mother's persecution. Then he becomes depressed because of his guilt. Along with the depressive position goes the feeling that he wants to make reparation for his wish to destroy, according to Mrs. Klein. She says these two early positions influence much of later behavior.

During our earliest months of life, the wish to kill is not felt as the actual wish to murder that we know as adults, but as the wish to devour or bite or chew up. For the mouth is then all we know as weapon. We are true little cannibals. When we reach the second or anal stage, we think of destroying someone in terms of degrading, soiling, or shaming (from this stage comes the expression "shit on you" as an epithet of hatred). It is only when we reach the last or genital stage that we think of destruction in terms of actual murder, such as strangling, knifing, axing, poisoning or what death you will. As Dr. Walter Stewart puts it, "Murder really begins as an intentional, knowledgeable act with the Oedipal conflict."

In discussing depression, Mrs. Klein declared there was "a close connection between the testing of reality in normal mourning and early processes of the mind."[2] "My contention is that the child goes through states of mind comparable to the mourning of the adult, or rather, that this early mourning is revived whenever grief is experienced in later life," she said.

She explained her theory of the depressive position:

The baby experiences depressive feelings which reach a climax just before, during and after weaning. This is the state of mind in the baby which I termed the "depressive position," and I suggested that it is a melancholia in *statu nascendi*. The object which is being mourned is the mother's breast and all that the breast and the milk have come to stand for in the infant's mind: namely, love, goodness and security. All these are felt by the baby to be lost, and lost as a result of his own uncontrollable greedy and destructive phantasies and impulses against his mother's breasts.

The circle of loved objects attacked in fantasy (and whose loss is therefore feared) widens as the child comes to know mixed feelings of love and hate for his father and either his actual brothers and sisters or fantasied brothers and sisters inside the mother's body, Mrs. Klein said.

The increase of love and trust and the diminishing of fears through happy experiences, help the baby step by step to overcome his depression and feeling of loss (mourning). They enable him to test his inner reality by means of outer reality. Through being loved and through the enjoyment and comfort he has in relation to people, his confidence in his own as well as in other people's goodness becomes strengthened, his hope that his "good" objects and his own ego can be saved and preserved increases, at the same time as his ambivalence and acute fears of internal destruction diminish.

Normally, the child passes through what Mrs. Klein calls "his infantile neurosis." Among other achievements, he arrives step by step at a good relation to people and to reality. She says, "I hold that this satisfactory relation to people depends upon his having succeeded in his struggle against the chaos inside him (the depressive position) and having securely established his 'good' internal objects."

She described "these feelings of sorrow and concern for the loved objects, the fears of losing them and the longing to regain them" as "pining."

She summed up:

In short—persecution (by "bad" objects) and the characteristic defences against it, on the one hand, and pining for the loved ("good") object, on the other, constitute the depressive position.

SPITZ: "THE ANACLITIC DEPRESSION"

Further study of depression in infants was made by Dr. René Spitz.[3] He followed up Abraham's theory of a primal depression and discovered another kind. He called it the "anaclitic depression." (Anaclitic means dependent, leaning on.)

Dr. Spitz reached a number of important conclusions about depression in the very young child. For one, to a child, the "loss" of his mother when she sinks into depression is not the same as her physical loss when she dies or disappears. Rather, it is an emotional loss:

. . . the mother, in changing her emotional attitude . . . radically changes the signals which identified her as good object for the child. Physically, she remains the same mother she was. Emotionally, the good mother, the libidinally invested object, the person whom the child loves, is lost.

The infant sees his mother in two images—the "good" and the "bad." The two images remain separate until, fusing good and bad, he looks at her as a human being, with the weaknesses and strengths of all humans. But the depressive mother blocks this normal development, Dr. Spitz held, as she withdraws from the child into her depression.

He explained:

The radical change of her emotional attitude transforms her into a bad object. While the good object invites the opportunities for action exchanges with the child, the mother who has withdrawn into her depression avoids and withholds them. The child is thus deprived of the opportunity to complete the fusion. In his need for action exchanges, he follows the mother into the depressive attitude.

Dr. Spitz studied depression in infants separated from their mothers after six months for a three-month period. This group was taken away from the mothers for "unavoidable external administrative reasons." The babies were born in a penal institution where the mothers were allowed care of them for the first six months, but then were not allowed to see the babies for the following three months.

The babies had "good" relations with their mothers during the first six months and their emotional and physical progress was normal. But in the following months, separated from their mothers, their behavior changed.

During the first month of separation, they became weepy, demanding, and clung to anyone who succeeded in making contact with them. In the eighth month, the weeping changed into wailing; they lost weight and their potential for development was arrested. In the ninth month, they refused contact with anyone, kept their faces rigid, lay prone in their cots most of the time, lost more weight and were unable to sleep at night. After this third month away from their mothers, the babies' facial rigidity was firmly established, the weeping was replaced by whimpering, and they were lethargic.

Dr. Spitz said that the symptoms and facial expression of these children were strongly reminiscent of those found in adults suffering from depression. But, "in view of the infant's incomplete psychic apparatus, in view of the special etiological [causal] factors which produce this syndrome, it was mandatory to distinguish it clearly from nosological [categorical] concepts of depression in adults. I therefore have called this syndrome anaclitic depression."

A very early depression due to separation from the mother presents other noteworthy peculiarities, Dr. Spitz said. When the child remains deprived of his mother without being provided an acceptable substitute for a period lasting longer than three to five months, further deterioration sets in.

But if during this transitional period the mother returns, the child will recover. However, even then it is doubtful if the recovery will be complete, in that the disturbance "will leave scars which will show in later years."

A necessary condition for the development of anaclitic depression is that prior to the separation the infant should have been "in *good* relations" with his mother. It is evidently more difficult to replace a satisfactory love object than an unsatisfactory one, Dr. Spitz noted. In the case of babies with "bad" relationships to their mother, only mild depressive results were seen.

"In these cases it would seem that any substitute was at least as good as the unsatisfactory biological mother," he explained.

When an infant is completely deprived of a mother, the results are different. This was shown in another study by Dr. Spitz, one which he described as "total deprivation."

If a baby is deprived for any length of time during his first year of life of *all* contact with his mother, he will show an increasingly serious deterioration which appears to be, in part at least, irreversible. The nature of the mother-child relationship, if any, that exists prior to the deprivation seems to have little influence on the course of what Dr. Spitz calls "the disease."

He observed this total deprivation and its consequences in a foundling home located outside the United States, which housed ninety-one infants. The children were breast-fed the first three months by their own mothers, or by one of the other mothers if the child's mother was not available. During this time, the babies had the appearance, and tested at the developmental level, of average normal children living in the same city.

After the third month, mother and child were separated. The infants remained in the foundling home, where they were adequately cared for in every bodily respect. They were given food, hygiene and medical care.

But one thing was lacking—emotional sustenance. A single nurse cared for twelve babies, hence each baby received very little individual attention.

"To put it drastically, they got approximately one tenth of the normal affective [emotional] supplies provided in the usual mother-child relationship," Dr. Spitz said.

Symptoms of anaclitic depression followed one another in rapid succession. After three months, the babies became completely passive, lying supine in their cots. Their faces were vacuous, their eye coordination defective and the expression on their faces often imbecilic. By the end of the second year their IQ stood at 45 per cent of the normal, at the level of the idiot. With few exceptions, they could not sit, stand, walk or talk. Some died, the will to live gone.

"Absence of mothering equals emotional starvation," concluded Dr. Spitz. "This leads to a progressive deterioration engulfing the child's whole person."

BOWLBY: "PROTEST, DESPAIR AND DETACHMENT"

The loss of maternal care in childhood was also studied by Dr. John Bowlby of the Tavistock Child Development Research Unit in London.[4] His research group studied what happened to children who lost their mothers between the ages of six months and six years.

He explained, as preliminary, that during the first months of life a baby learns to discriminate among the figures that pass before his crib and develops a strong liking for one figure, usually his mother. Throughout the last half of his first year, and during the whole of his second and third, he becomes closely attached to his mother. He is "content in her company and distressed in her absence." He protests even momentary separations. From his first birthday on, other figures, such as a father or brother or sister, may also become important but not as important as his mother.

Most children suffer little disruption of these first attachments in their early years. But a minority, whose mothers have died or deserted them, or could not take care of them for one reason or another, are put into hospitals, institutions or foster homes. Or they are handed from one relative to another. It was this group which Dr. Bowlby and his researchers studied.

They observed the behavior of healthy infants two and three years old, placed for limited stays in residential nurseries or hospital wards. There they were cared for by strangers, "a succession of unfamiliar people," for various periods of time. These children were then returned home to parents.

The child who was fifteen to thirty months of age when

the separation occurred, who had a reasonably secure relationship with his mother and had not previously been parted from her, showed "a predictable sequence of behavior."

Such a child went through three phases when separated from his mother—protest, despair and detachment. In Dr. Bowlby's words:

At first with tears and anger he demands his mother back and seems hopeful he will succeed in getting her. This phase of Protest may last several days. Later he becomes quieter, but to the discerning eye it is clear that as much as ever he remains preoccupied with his absent mother and still yearns for her return; but his hopes have faded and he is in the phase of Despair. Often these 2 phases alternate: hope turns to despair and despair to renewed hope. Eventually, however, a greater change occurs. He seems to forget his mother so that when she comes for him he remains curiously uninterested in her, and may seem even not to recognize her. This is the phase of Detachment.

In each of the three phases the child is prone to tantrums and episodes of destructive behavior, often of a "disquietingly violent kind."

The child's behavior on return home depends on the phase reached during his period of separation. Usually, for a while, he is unresponsive and undemanding. To what degree and for how long depends on the length of the separation and the frequency of the visits made by his mother. When he has not been visited for a few weeks or months and has reached the early stages of detachment, it is likely he will be unresponsive anywhere from an hour to a day or more. But when the detachment does break, his emotions will be intense.

"There is a storm of feeling, intense clinging and, whenever his mother leaves him, even for a moment, acute anxiety and rage," reported Dr. Bowlby. For weeks or months, his mother may be the target of demands for her presence and angry reproaches when she is away.

But when the infant has been separated from his mother for more than six months, or when separations have been so repeated that he has reached an advanced stage of detachment, there is danger he may remain detached and never recover his affection for his mother or father.

In relating such behavior to adults who are depressed, Dr. Bowlby observed, "There is, indeed, good reason to believe that the sequence of responses—Protest, Despair and Detachment—is a sequence that, in one variant or another, is characteristic of all forms of mourning."

Following an unexpected loss there seems to be a phase of protest in which the one who is bereaved strives, either in deed, thought or feeling, to recover the lost loved one at the same time as he also reproaches it for the desertion. During this period and during the following phase of despair, feelings of love and hate are mixed. Mood and action vary from an immediate expectancy, expressed in an angry demand for the person's return, to a despair expressed in "subdued pining" or not expressed at all. Though alternating hope and despair may continue, eventually there develops some measure of emotional detachment from the one who is lost. Then follows acceptance of permanent absence.

This Dr. Bowlby calls "healthy mourning" when it occurs in an adult. It becomes unhealthy, or pathological, in a child because it occurs at a time of life when he is too young to handle his deep feelings of loss, needing a loving attachment. As a result, the mourning processes that lead to detachment in an adult are premature. They take a course that if it occurred in older children and adults would be regarded as pathological.

Dr. Bowlby emphasizes that anger is usually the first and the immediate, "perhaps invariable," response to loss of a loved one. Instead of anger being a sign that mourning is running a pathological course, "a view suggested by Freud and rather commonly held," the evidence makes it clear, Dr. Bowlby maintained, that anger, including anger at the one who is lost, is an integral part of the reaction of grief. This anger appears to serve the purpose of adding "punch" to strenuous efforts both to recover the lost one and to dissuade it from deserting again. These efforts are the hallmarks of the first phase of mourning.

The acceptance that there must be anger "appears crucial" for an understanding of mental illness, he declared. As for the tendency to regard such anger as pathological, Dr. Bowlby said:

> I believe this to be profoundly mistaken. So far from being pathological, the evidence suggests that the overt expression of this powerful urge, unrealistic and hopeless though it may be, is a necessary condition for mourning to run a healthy course. Only after every effort has been made to recover the lost object, it seems, is the individual in a mood to admit defeat and to orient himself afresh to a world from which the loved object is accepted as irretrievably missing. Protest, including an angry demand for the object's return and reproach against it for deserting, is as much a part of the *adult's* response to loss, especially a sudden loss, as of the young child's.

He pointed out that even animals act this way. This, he said, suggests that such responses have "ancient biological roots." He cited the case of a male chimpanzee who, after his mate died, made repeated efforts to arouse her lifeless body. He yelled with rage and expressed his anger by trying to pull out the short hairs on his head. Then he cried and mourned. As time wore on, he became more closely attached to his keeper, showing anger whenever the keeper left him.

It is not difficult to understand why the reactions of anxiety and protest, despair and disorganization, detachment and reorganization are the rule for both animals and humans, Dr. Bowlby said. In the wild, to lose contact with the family is extremely dangerous, especially for the young, who cannot protect themselves against attack by enemies. It is in the interest of the survival of the individual, both for his own safety and so he will live to reproduce the species, that there be strong bonds tying together the members of a family. This requires that at every separation, however brief, a person or animal respond by "an immediate, automatic and strong effort" both to recover the lost one, especially if it is the member to whom attachment is closest (usually the mother), and to discourage that member from ever leaving again.

For this reason, Dr. Bowlby suggested, "the inherited determinants of behavior (often termed instinctual) have evolved in such a way that the standard responses to loss of a loved one are always urges first to recover it and then to scold it."

If neither the futile effort to recover the lost object nor angry reproaches against it for deserting are signs of pathology, in what ways does pathological mourning differ from healthy mourning, he asked.

He answered by saying that one of the characteristics of pathological mourning is the inability to express openly the wish to recover the lost object and to express anger at it. Instead of open expression, "which though stormy and fruitless leads on to a healthy outcome," the urges to recover and reproach, with all their mixed feelings of love and hate, become "split off and repressed." They continue as "active systems" within the person. Unable to find open and direct expression, they influence feeling and behavior "in strange and distorted ways."

Dr. Bowlby mentioned a case reported by Dr. Helene Deutsch, in which a young man in his early thirties came to her for analysis even though he appeared to possess no apparent problems. But he had "a wooden and affectionless character," according to Dr. Bowlby. The young man could not fall in love, was unable to form friendships, felt no interest in anyone. "There was no endeavor and no disappointment . . . There were no reactions of grief at the loss of individuals near to him, no unfriendly feelings and no aggressive impulses."

When he was five years old his mother had died. He had accepted her loss without any show of feeling. He could not remember any events prior to her death. But during his analysis he described how, after she died, he would leave his bedroom door open "in the hope that a large dog would come to him, be very kind to him, and fulfill all his wishes." He remembered a dog he once owned who left her puppies alone and helpless when she died shortly after their birth. Dr. Bowlby pointed out that the young man's memories and feelings about his mother had disappeared from consciousness, displaced onto the dog. Following his mother's death, instead of being able to express a wish for her return and anger at her desertion, his mourning had moved directly to the phase of detachment. He had skipped the first two necessary phases of anger and despair.

In doing so, Dr. Bowlby said, the young man's yearning and anger had become locked inside him. They were potentially active but shut off from the world. Only the remainder of his personality had been left free for further development. As a result, he grew up "gravely impoverished."

The findings of a number of analysts suggest that such a person has to return emotionally to the early phases of mourning, with their feelings of love and hate, before he "can be restored to a life of feeling and attachment," says Dr. Bowlby.

If the early phases are not passed through, the experience of loss does not "quietly fade," as has been suggested by Anna Freud, Dr. Bowlby said. Nor will there be "a simple forgetting." Instead, the feelings of yearning and anger remain latent, ready to become active again at high intensity when circumstances change. This was shown by the children who were restored to their mothers after separation and clung with an almost violent attachment.

Thus, what happens in childhood mourning, and in the pathological mourning of later years, Dr. Bowlby showed, is that *"the development of defense processes is accelerated. As a result, the urges to recover and to reproach the lost object have no chance to be extinguished and instead persist, with consequences that are serious"* (Italics added).

Two psychic processes come into play, "fixation" and "repression." A child will remain "fixated" on his lost mother as both his urges to recover and reproach her, and his mixed emotions of love and hate connected with these urges, undergo repression. (Incidentally, the word "hang-up," now so popular, is a perfect description of what psychoanalysts mean by "fixated.")

Another defensive process, closely related to an alternative to repression, also occurs following a loss, Dr. Bowlby pointed out. It is called "splitting of the ego." One part of the personality, "secret but conscious," denies that the person is really lost. It maintains, instead, either that there is still communication or that the lost one will soon be recovered. Simultaneously, another part of the personality admits to the world that the person is irretrievably lost. These two parts seem incompatible but they can coexist in the mind over the years. Such splits of the ego, as well as repression, may lead to emotional illness, Dr. Bowlby added.

A child's ego is not as strong as an adult's. He cannot reason and he will react more violently to a loss. Dr. Bowlby believes that often later emotional illness is an expression of early pathological mourning that has been repressed.

He pointed out that in the young child the experience of separation from the mother is especially apt to evoke psychological processes of a kind that "are as crucial for psychopathology as are inflammation and its resulting scar tissue to physiopathology." This does not mean, he added, that a crippling of personality is the inevitable result of separation. But it does mean that, as in the case, for instance, of rheumatic fever, scar tissue is all too often formed which, in later life, leads to more or less severe inability to function.

Dr. Bowlby's conclusions hold many implications for our understanding of pathological depression. It would appear that there is a strong link between the emotional disturbances of later life in regard to loss and the losses that have occurred in childhood. Dr. Bowlby shows that the defensive process following childhood loss is not an *alternative* to mourning, but *a part of* mourning. What is pathological is not the defensive process in itself, but the prematurity of the third phase as the first two phases are consigned to the unconscious without having been experienced fully. (They have been *repressed,* an automatic action, rather than *suppressed,* a conscious one.)

In other words, the depressed adult suffers from *not* having been able to go through the natural processes of mourning. He has repressed his rage at the loved one for what he considers abandonment, and also repressed his despair. He has not been able to reach the healthy goal of detachment and acceptance. The *depression* rises from the *repression* of the first two phases.

Dr. Bowlby's findings also suggest that we may fly too swiftly through the processes of mourning for the little separations that occur in childhood—the unexplained absences of a mother, and every crisis that feels like a desertion, such as weaning, toilet training and the birth of a brother or sister (when she leaves to go to the hospital and returns with a hated rival). If the anger, then despair, then detachment, do not proceed in that order, gradually allowing us to accept each phase and progress to the next, perhaps we will somehow mourn the rest of our life, not knowing for what.

In analysis, the patient is often able to finally feel within himself a devastating rage at an early desertion or death which, up to then, he was unable to feel. Then follows the devastating despair. Then proper detachment takes place.

MAHLER: DEPRESSION FOLLOWING NORMAL SEPARATION

Most of us do not face actual physical separation from a mother but have to adjust to a psychic separation, one inherent in normal growth. This process has been intensively studied by Dr. Margaret Mahler. She has observed how mothers and babies affect each other, as far as separation is concerned, in a research project, "Study of Normal Separation-Individuation," conducted for eight years at the Masters Children's Center in New York City. [5, 6]

The death of the mother, or her physical absence, is an infrequent occurrence as compared to the widespread existence among mothers of depressive moods or depressive illness, Dr. Mahler points out. She adds, "Thus, it must be loss in fantasy, that is to say *intrapsychic conflict* of a particular type of constellation [that affects the child]."

Every infant has to face giving up the belief that he is one with his mother, which he actually is when inside her womb. He has to be able to bear becoming separate from her. Gradually, he must relinquish the fantasy of "symbiotic omnipotence," one that allows him to believe that both he and his mother are all-powerful.

As an infant matures physically, he also matures psychically, which means he should successfully start to give up his emotional attachment to his mother so he may eventually establish his own identity.

During this crucial time in an infant's life, his mother, if she is emotionally able, "functions as a protective shield," according to Dr. Mahler. She takes care of him and makes sure he does not hurt himself either physically or psychically. She rescues him from any situation that may produce anxiety or fear.

There exists what Dr. Mahler calls a "mutual cueing of mother and child." The child conveys to his mother his needs, physically and emotionally. She in turn conveys to him the feeling that she has understood what he wants and will take care of him.

If there is a significant lack of acceptance by the mother of the child, she misses his cues and in turn does not furnish him with enough assurances of comfort and love. This "deficit in mothering" may result in a diminution of the infant's self-esteem. This may be followed by depression, Dr. Mahler suggests.

She reports that small children who show "the basic depressive mood" do not possess much confidence and self-esteem. Too great a portion of their aggression goes into defenses that ward off rage and a fear of annihilating the mother through fantasies. At the same time, they struggle to restore the state of oneness with the mother, a state from which they should be emerging.

It is Dr. Mahler's hypothesis that if the spurt to grow

physically and learn to sit up, crawl and walk, as well as to learn how to think, takes place in infants concomitantly with a lag in their emotional readiness to function separately from the mother, there will be "organismic panic."

The mental content of this panic is not readily discernible because the child is still unable to talk and cannot communicate (although the child has fantasies as one way of combating the panic). Bodily maturation will proceed but healthy emotional development has been hindered, thwarted or blocked. This may occur to such an intense degree that the child becomes psychotic, unable to move out of his fantasy world.

Dr. Mahler found that whereas most mothers, except the very psychotic, take care of their baby's physical needs during the phase of complete bodily dependence (until about nine to ten months of age), the capability for maintaining the infant's "basic trust" is different, both qualitatively and quantitatively, among average mothers and their babies, even under normal circumstances.

It is easy to see, she says, that some infants have a somewhat lesser "sending power" (faulty or less cueing ability) than others. Also, that some mothers are less attuned than others to their infant's primitive emotional needs. The child may have to exert himself quite a bit to obtain from the mother what he needs.

She emphasizes the point that a child must be ready emotionally to separate himself from his mother in order to develop *psychically,* even though his limbs will perform as they should and he has a high I.Q. If he is not emotionally ready for the separation, he may resent it. He may live in perpetual fury at having to undertake more than he is ready for. Then, because of this fury, he will feel guilty and become depressed. This may be the basis for all later depression.

The study shows that the small child who gives evidence of "the basic, depressive mood" lacks enough self-esteem to adequately master reality. Too great a part of his energy is being used for psychic mechanisms which serve to ward off a sense of loss. They also signal a wish

to return to a former state of well-being, which to him
means oneness with his mother.

Dr. Mahler believes that the contribution to early depression of "the double trauma" of toilet training and the
discovery (much earlier than has been generally
thought) of the anatomical difference between the
sexes must be emphasized. However, she maintains that
the early conflicts inherent in accepting the psychic loss
of the mother are but compounded by "the emotion-
ridden symbolic significance of the phase of toilet training
which follows, and by the advent of the castration anxiety
of the phallic phase of psychosexual development." Contrary to some psychoanalysts, she holds that the
birth of a brother or sister, if it coincides with these
earlier conflicts, while significant, is not the original cause
of conflict. It does not generate by itself the depressive
mood, or the proclivity to depressive illness. Rather, the
birth of a rival only accentuates, dramatizes and com-
pounds "the basically negative mood predisposition of
the child."

She makes a distinction between "sadness with psychic
content," a sadness which has an imaginative quality, and
the earlier, transient physiological reactions of pain to the
trauma of weaning or longer-lasting bodily distress, which
a later pervasive depressive mood may or may not com-
pound.

The depressive response, with or without a generally
angry mood, was observed in girls "definitely more" than
in boys, Dr. Mahler reports. She explains, "Their anger
about and disappointment with mother having not given
them the penis could be convincingly traced in several
cases."

Dr. Mahler's work is important because it shows, with
specific examples, what may happen if a child is unable
to progress successfully, in an emotional sense, through
the first years of life because he has not received enough
emotional sustenance to help him separate successfully
from his mother and achieve a sense of self-esteem. As a
result, depression and the various defenses erected against

it may set in and form a pattern that will persist in later life.

JACOBSON AND OTHERS: DEPRESSION UNDER A MICROSCOPE

Another psychoanalyst who has studied the nature of depression is Dr. Edith Jacobson.[7] She reported that patients who in early childhood had lost one or both parents "showed the emotional scars left by their infantile psychic injury. In most of them the old wounds had never healed." Their ability to relate to others was seriously affected. They suffered from depressive states and other symptoms in which the traumatic experiences of infancy played a decisive role.

She theorized that children experience the loss of a parent not only in terms of loss of love or of a love object, "but also as a severe narcissistic injury, a castration." (To the unconscious, death is castration and castration, death.)

Since children, in their first years of life, depend on parents for their supply of self-esteem, to be motherless, fatherless, an orphan or an adopted child is felt to be "utterly degrading," Dr. Jacobson said. She added:

The fact that in such children the hostile and derogatory feelings caused by their losses are so commonly diverted to the surviving parent or the parent substitutes, while the lost object becomes glorified, tends to raise that object's narcissistic value and meaning to the point of turning it into the most precious part of the self which has been lost and must be recovered.

This explains why such children refuse to accept, and struggle against identifying with, their surviving (to them, castrated) parent or the parent substitute. In other words, it is not unusual to hear a child blame a mother for his father having left the home, no matter what the facts may be.

Dr. Jacobson has advanced the theory that too early a

disappointment in parents will cause depression.[8] She describes "disappointment" as an experience which comes about when promises and expectations of gratification are not fulfilled. She states that oral frustration, in particular the state of severe and lasting hunger, seems to be the earliest forerunner of profound disappointment "such as comes about later by being hit by the loss of a most valuable object."

In a state of severe disappointment, one finds "the feeling of blank, empty hopelessness, of nothingness, often accompanied by the sensation of physical emptiness . . . ," she says.

As the infant grows, a process of disillusionment sets in, caused by increasing disappointments inflicted by the parents. These force the child "to a critical revision of the illusionary parental images." Whether this process of disillusionment has a constructive or destructive effect on the development of the child's ego and his sense of reality "depends less on the severity of the disappointments in the parents than on the stage at which they set in," Dr. Jacobson holds.

If the child meets with "decisive disappointments" at a time when his infantile ego has asserted itself to some extent, disillusion in the parents results in a realistic evaluation of the parents and the world, as well as of himself, which is the prerequisite of the normal formation of the ego.

But the child who has been disappointed too early cannot use his disillusionment in the service of the development of his ego. On the contrary, he "must get involved in the collapse of his world of magic." Instead of acquiring a realistic picture of the world, the child may swing from an optimistic to a pessimistic illusion which again distorts reality, Dr. Jacobson states.

The parents, once omnipotent gods, as they pass through the grind of devaluating criticism, may turn into bad, hostile, punishing beings not only deprived of their divine power but appearing bad in a deprecatory way: low, defiled, empty, castrated . . . evil as well as worthless.

As the ego of the infant takes part in the downfall of the godlike parents, their destruction becomes identical with self-deflation and self-destruction. The child will respond, from then on, to any disappointment with a narcissistic hurt. He will also become sensitized for direct attacks on his narcissism or for failure in his adjustment to the world. He will react to them as to disappointments coming from a love object.

This creates an interaction of disappointment and narcissistic injury causing and affecting each other, whose beginnings one can observe in connection with cleanliness training, Dr. Jacobson maintains. She cites a case, a thirty-six-year-old writer whose earliest recollection of a depression led back to the age of three. He recalled being in the bathroom, sitting on "a chamber pot," feeling alone and remote from his mother, who was taking care of the other children, particularly his next older brother, who was her pet. Eventually, she turned to him, lifted him from the pot, looked in and said derogatorily, "Nothing of course." His older brother smiled at his humiliation. He remembers vividly the dull, empty, desperate hopelessness connected with the feeling of utter worthlessness, typical of this time of his life and of his later depressions. On the surface this scene seemed to revolve around the rejection by his mother because of her child's failure to "produce," said Dr. Jacobson. In the analysis, however, his stubborn refusal to "produce" was repeated in his writing and love problems, and represented "a vindictive and at the same time masochistic response to his mother's neglect." She added, "Since she does not care for him, he cannot give her anything. As she appears worthless to him, his anal present loses its value and becomes dirt. The ensuing rejection on her part crushes the infantile ego all the more and causes further disappointment, so that a vicious circle arises."

Severe disillusionment in the parents during the first years of life "crushes" the infantile ego on the one hand, and, on the other, may start the formation of conscience at an earlier stage than usual.

Dr. Sandor Lorand, who has studied and treated the depressed person, found as a rule that his conflict centered not only around the mother but all the members of the family responsible for her loss in early childhood, although the mother was the most important.[9] "The patient's memory retains from the very earliest years the frustrations by the mother; it is this frustrating, threatening, punishing attitude of hers which stands out most conspicuously in the patient's recollections, overshadowing the mother's love," he says.

He adds that when the father, brothers and sisters interfere with the child's wish for sole possession of the mother's love, "an unlimited jealousy" is aroused in the child against the other members of the family. This then becomes responsible for the tremendous envy which is so notable a characteristic of depression.

Thus, aggression against the world is aggression displaced from the early years in which the "world" was mother, father, brothers and sisters, states Dr. Lorand.

He also found that depression in an adult always presupposes a psychically painful early childhood which "forms the fertile soil in which the later adult depression grows." Also, it becomes clear during an analysis, he said, "that the adult situation that precipitated the current depression is emotionally identical with the patient's childhood environment."

In the analyses of depressed men and women he found they all "had endured experiences which caused severe infantile neuroses, which may be looked upon as the earliest depression."

Melancholia is described as "a great despairing cry for love," by Dr. Sandor Rado.[10] The melancholiac blames himself for the loss of his love and thinks his aggressive feelings are responsible for that loss, Dr. Rado says.

He calls "the torments of hunger" the mental precursor of later "punishments." He declares that by way of the discipline of punishment they come to be the main mechanism of self-punishment, which in depression assumes "such a fatal significance." (Some mothers as punishment will deprive children of desserts or other sweets.)

". . . Drinking at the mother's breasts remains the

radiant image of unremitting, forgiving love," he says. "It is certainly no mere chance that the Madonna nursing the Child has become the emblem of a mighty rebellion and thereby the emblem of a whole epoch of our Western civilization."

Dr. Ludwig Eidelberg, who has written about depression, states that after the child discovers he and his parents are not omnipotent, he may try to save his megalomania by attempting to play the role of the lover and the beloved, the winner and the loser at the same time.[11]

In other words, in depression, the wish to kill is turned on the self as the self plays both the one who feels deprived of love and the one he feels has deprived him of love. Thus we can see how, in suicide, the one who kills himself believes he is also killing the one who has abandoned him.

Dr. Eidelberg also raises the question as to whether a baby suffers a "narcissistic mortification" at the same time he is being instinctually gratified, when he is first fed by his mother.[12] He takes, as example, the mother who "pushes a spoonful of porridge into the mouth of a child that up to then has been acquainted only with the milk bottle, and forces the child to swallow the food." The child has been deprived of food for a sufficiently long time to be hungry. Under these circumstances, it seems justified to assume, he says, that the mother's feeding of the child "produces an instinctual gratification" (he is no longer hungry) and "a narcissistic mortification" (a pleasure to which he has been accustomed has been suddenly taken away from him and he is forced to do something different).

Many children, on discovering this new source of pleasure, give up all resistance, and allow themselves to be fed. But others resist violently. Dr. Eidelberg points out the difference between a mother who "half playfully touches the child's mouth with the spoon; she confines herself to calling the child's attention to the porridge, and permits him to hold the spoon and smear his face," and a mother who "energetically pushes the food into the child's mouth, suppresses any resistance, sometimes repeats the feeding before the child had a chance to become hungry again." Assuming that the oral gratification is equal in the two cases, the amount of "narcissistic mortification" suffered by the two infants is certainly not the same, he points out.

Even if, in the case of the first child, mortification is not entirely avoided, it is not violently imposed as in the second, he states. He lists three different types of behavior on the part of a child in such an instance: the hesitating child, who is apparently unable to make up his mind about the food and leaves the decision to the adult; the good child, who shows that he accepts and desires the food; and the bad child, who energetically resists feeding.

The amount of mortification suffered by the child can be linked to the depression in that feeling mortified may make the child angry, hate the mother and wish to kill her, which then leads to guilt and depression.

An eloquent description of the depressed person, plus further understanding of what happens within him, is given by Dr. Georg Gero.[13] In his study of what he terms "the depressive obsessional character," who seems to be "in a continuous state of being on one's guard against oneself, a complete inability to break loose," he says of such persons:

Their impulses are always reined in. They feel in themselves something excessive and passionate which they fear without knowing what it is. They are afraid to lose control, lest these dark passions should carry them away.

Abnormal sadistic impulses cause these defensive measures. Such people suffer from a chronic damming up of the feeling of aggression:

On the one hand their repressed feelings of aggression are tremendously strong, on the other hand their excessively strict super-ego does not permit them even innocent acts of aggression. Always held back, continually hurt, they long for revenge, but they can never satisfy these feelings.

Talking of the need for masochistic punishment, Dr. Gero says:

Every sexual impulse, all sexual interest, is suppressed in the child, punished and condemned as something ugly, dirty and dangerous. Sexuality is wrapped in deep and oppressive mystery. Out of this atmosphere arise the masochistic phantasies. What else is left to the child than masochistic and sadistic frightening phantasies when it feels sexual excitement? The child does not know that sexuality is pleasurable and beautiful, for his upbringing prevents this knowledge and forces other conceptions on him. These masochistic phantasies have besides the function of unburdening the child's conscience.

Speaking of one patient, he said that she not only lacked actual nourishment in her infancy and later childhood (she grew up in Europe during World War II when food was scarce) but she was also "starved of love." He explained, "In depressive and melancholic types being fed means being loved. Being fed means not only the isolated act of alimentation, but the feeling of being loved, cared for, wrapped up in an atmosphere of affectionate warmth and safety. And hunger means loneliness, being thrust out, forsaken."

Why cannot the depressed person realize his wish to be loved? Dr. Gero explains that such a person is incapable of "a genital love-relationship," one in which the infantile wishes for warmth and tenderness may be fulfilled, as well as adult sexuality. This type of relationship constitutes for the adult the only possibility "to safeguard the inheritance of infancy." People for whom this path is not open, "the neurotic," suffer from an insoluble contradiction. They long for something unattainable—they are grown up but want to be loved like children. "In other words," Dr. Gero explains technically, "the anxieties overshadowing the genital sexuality press the libido back into the pregenital positions. Thus these demands gain an uncanny force."

Being capable of "genital sex," psychoanalytically

speaking, means you are unafraid of your sexual desire
for an appropriate member of the opposite sex. This in
turn means that you do not have unconscious fantasies
about sex as an assaultive, destructive act, as did the
woman patient of whom Dr. Gero spoke. He said for
this very depressed young woman genital sexuality
meant

a bloody uncanny thing, coitus was a great danger, the man
an enemy who wanted to do something terrible to her with his
penis. She could not give herself to a man; she was incapable
of loving . . . She could not be loved like a grown-up woman,
but like a child she wanted to be protected, warmed and
spoiled. The repeated disappointments she had to undergo
plunged her into depression. "Nobody loves me whatever I do,
nobody understands me, I am lonely and forsaken—as I was
in my childhood," this was the simplified formula of her
depression.

Her analysis succeeded in overcoming her anxieties, in
destroying her fantasies about sex, and brought "liberation." She became capable of loving someone, no longer
afraid of sex.

In the study of depression, even the very first hours in
an infant's life are being observed. Dr. Margaret Fries
reported thirty-five years ago on the relationship between
mother and baby during the first ten days, as a way of
understanding the child's later development. She studied
infants attending the Well Baby Clinic at the New York
Infirmary. By six to eight weeks, the babies had already
showed patterns of behavior.[14]

She found that "the most important single factor, for
the young infant, is the emotional adjustment of the
parents and especially the mother." The mother's attitude
is conveyed to the infant directly through everything she
does, "not only nursing, but also undressing, holding,
tucking him in the crib, washing him. Her fingers, arms
and voice produce comfort or discomfort."

"The dependent newborn is, so to say, enveloped in a

twenty-four hour emotional atmosphere, but how he will respond depends upon his own make-up," she holds.

It is the interaction of the total environment with the total infant that is responsible not only for the child's future integrated development but the mother's as well, Dr. Fries believes. Especially important is the amount of gratification or anxiety experienced by both. The mother contributes the opportunities for the infant to satisfy his needs, but his ability and the way he uses these contribute to her emotional state. This is true communication between the two and it is present before words are used, she states.[15]

The maximum amount of gratification "in every act of the day" by the mother, with the minimum accompanying amount of anxiety, will lead to a more emotionally secure child.

What the infant needs, in Dr. Fries's opinion, is friendly, warm, understanding parents to help him meet the small, necessary daily frustrations of reality. The more of a sense of reality he gains, the easier his later life will be because the less he will live in fantasy.

Thus, when faced with the question as to why some adults mourn a loss and are done with it, while others sink into a depression so deep they must kill themselves, we see that the answer lies in the whole of each one's life, starting with the very first days of infancy.

Depression is rooted not in any one event of later life, although the event may set it off, but in childhood. Its beginnings are at birth, perhaps even in the womb. Pioneer research at the Fels Institute shows that if a pregnant woman is depressed this will affect the physical and emotional reactions of the fetus.

In growing up, not only do we have our own powerful impulses which we must learn to control but our mother's and father's emotions with which to contend. If a child lives in the aura of a parent's depression, he is likely to react to what otherwise might not be crippling crises as though they were a matter of life and death. As Dr. Elisabeth R. Geleerd says:

In order not to lose his parents' love, the child adopts their repressions, denials, reaction formations, etc. . . . Only by taking over a considerable part of his parents' neurotic ways can he join the human community. It is a paradox that the human being, in order not to become isolated from other humans, in order to communicate with others, has to learn their faulty ways of dealing with conflicts.[16]

In a depressed atmosphere, the frustrations every child must learn to endure may appear to him unbearable—his weaning, when he is deprived of his mother's breast, or if bottle fed, of the comfort of her arms; toilet training, when he is deprived of the pleasure of relieving his inner pressures whenever and wherever he wishes; the birth of a brother or sister, rival for his mother's love; momentary separation from his mother, which looms as a terror time.

The depressed mother is unlikely to encourage her child, who starts off being dependent on her, to become independent. When he is separated from her, or frustrated by her, which inevitably he must be, he will hate her with a vengeance that far exceeds that of the less dependent child. This hate brings excessive guilt, then depression, as he turns the hate inward, so that when she eventually dies, he is apt to punish himself through even deeper deprivation.

Babies believe their mother to be perfect, even though she may be a combination of Lucrezia Borgia and Lady Macbeth. They cannot afford to be angry at her and thus risk losing her love. So they learn to conceal their anger when she frustrates them in any way (babies cannot bear even realistic frustration). They repress their anger, hoping thus to eliminate it. Instead, they indulge in fantasy. If they are hungry and their mother is late with food, they suck their thumb, believing this will stem their hunger. Or they may urinate or defecate, venting their anger more harmlessly than piercing the air with raging screams and bringing their mother's wrath down on their heads. Mothers and fathers have been known to kill a screaming baby, so uncontrolled was their rage.

Intense hatred does not stay buried in babies any more than in adults. It may erupt in fantasy as well as deed. One fantasy of a child is that it's all the mother's fault. The child's reasoning goes, "She is late with my food so she hates me and wants to kill me. So it is all right for me to hate her and want to kill her. But if she knows I feel that way, she may kill me, or refuse to bring me any more food." The child cannot possibly understand that his mother may be a very busy woman, that she tries her best to know and meet his needs. Nor can he know that his demands are unreasonable, that the most perfect mother in the world could not satisfy them.

He must think her perfect—and he must also think her a wicked, wicked witch. Thus he is bound to be confused, and angry. To ease his anger, the baby uses fantasy, one of his psychic means of survival (thank heaven there are many such psychic means or none of us would live beyond the first six months). And that's where depression begins.

Dr. Martin Grotjahn has written an eloquent passage describing the fears of childhood and adulthood.[17] He says, ". . . the greatest mental dread of a child: that he may someday lose control of his bad thoughts and they may suddenly get loose like a swarm of bats from a cave after sunset. We live in constant dread that our unconscious may find its way to consciousness and may overwhelm our controls, then Mr. Hyde would overpower Dr. Jekyll and would do all the bad things we had hoped were safely repressed a long time ago."

Thus, part of us is apt to feel, "If I ever let go, I will destroy myself and everyone around me. I will steal, use profane language, rob, have sex with everybody, man, woman and child, kill my mother and father and sisters and brothers and wife and children." This is the fantasy of uncontrolled violence, the monster fantasy. Who is the monster? Ourselves, of course. Our own unbridled, primitive passions.

One way we guard against letting loose our violence is to become depressed. And one time we might feel most depressed as a child is when our mother leaves us, for whatever reason.

Anna Freud, who has studied and treated children, worked in England during World War II, using the knowledge of maternal deprivation to help ease the anxiety of children taken from their homes in the cities during the blitz.

During her experiences in treating children and adults, she found, as her father had said, that the depressed mother generates in her child depressive tendencies. The child "follows her [the mother] into the depressive mood," according to Miss Freud. This process was not an imitation of the mother. The depressed mood in the child was a response to the emotional climate, which infected his psyche as a germ would his body.[18] (One son felt his mother liked him only when he was depressed—when he was in the opposite, or manic stage, she could not manage him—so he unconsciously sank into a depression much of the time.)

A dramatic illustration of how a depressed mother conveyed her depression to her son and daughter and the tragedy that ensued is described by Dr. Alexander Gralnick, medical director of High Point Hospital, in Port Chester, New York, in what has become known as the case of the Carrington family.[19] The phrase "psychosis of association," which is Dr. Gralnick's, is also referred to as *folie à deux*. In such instances, two, three or, as in the Carrington family, four (her husband also was involved) persons become so necessary to each other emotionally that they prefer to destroy themselves rather than give up the involvements.

A child may sense in a depressed mother her unconscious wish to kill. A number of analysts have written of the effect of the unconscious, unspoken delinquent wishes of the parent upon the behavior of children, who act out what their parents unconsciously wish. Several analysts have pointed out that in the legend of Oedipus, the tragic act was originally set in motion by the parents' attempts to kill Oedipus when he was a baby, to prevent the prophecy of the Delphic oracle from coming true.

The average parent may hate his child at times, not enough to murder him, but merely to wish him temporarily out of the way, or possibly regret, for the shade of a moment, that the child was born. Children sense this hatred and respond with fear (because they are not being loved one hundred per cent) and hatred. Some children have killed parents, although this occurs far more rarely than a parent killing a child.

Incest may play a more important role than has previously been suspected in the killing of children, according to Roger O. Olive, chief psychologist at the Ionia State Hospital in Michigan.[20] He reported that in 1963 the incidence of incest was estimated to be one in every 500,000 persons. Now, he said, the estimate is one for each 1,000. "We also estimate that one out of every ten children seen at community child-care facilities is involved in incestuous behavior," he declared.

In a study conducted by him at the Ionia State Hospital, 40 per cent of the women he questioned who had killed their children admitted incestuous experiences. He added, "Further review of the case history and interview materials among the filicidal women may result in figures even higher than the 40 per cent one."

It might be a fairly accurate guess to suppose that murderers were unable as children to work through the first two phases of the depressive process as outlined by Dr. Bowlby—protest and despair. Take, as example, Richard Speck, who murdered eight student nurses in Chicago in July, 1966. His own words told how, as a child, he felt deep hatred for his stepfather. If ever Freud's point needed to be proved, that in the unconscious every murderer is killing one or all members of his childhood family, Speck proved it. He told a Chicago Cook County Jail psychiatrist, "There was blood on my hands . . . I killed sixteen people . . . the eight girls and my family."

In his unconscious, there were another eight victims, consisting of three brothers (one had died), four sisters (some older, some younger) and either his mother or father (his stepfather would be a substitute for his father). One acute prognostician, before Speck was even caught, predicted that the murderer, if found, would be likely to have a large number of sisters.

Dr. Ner Littner, a Chicago psychoanalyst, interviewed Speck at the request of the Public Defender in the Cook County Jail on February 4, 1967, spending four hours with him. He described Speck as quite cooperative. "He joked and smiled several times when we chatted about inconsequential matters," said Dr. Littner. "However, basically he presented a pleasant surface facade which covered over a real inability to relate to me or to make emotional contact. In addition to this emotional isolation I sensed an undercurrent of depression throughout."

Speck's life was filled with violence. He had attacked his mother several times, once beating her up in a rage when he was eighteen. He had been taking drugs, he told Dr. Littner. He had tried to kill himself twice, the first time when he was sixteen, driving his stepfather's car, and again just before he was caught.

He told Dr. Littner that he had always cried a lot (a sign of depression) and never was able to control tears coming to his eyes, especially when high on drugs.

He worried about shipping out on a boat for fifty or sixty days because it meant being away so much from his mother and he would miss her a great deal, he said. It had always bothered him whenever he was away from his mother because he would get so homesick. This, at the age of twenty-five.

Dr. Littner, in his report, stated that Speck's major relationship "is an unusual closeness to his mother." His other relationships were with "depreciated" women; he married one he knew was pregnant by another man and who was promiscuous.

"He has experienced an unusual sense of closeness to his mother," said Dr. Littner. "He considers her his closest friend. He has been extremely homesick when away from her. He could not tolerate being away from her at age sixteen years and so returned home then."

In Speck there was great dependence on his mother, an inability to accept any separation, and intense impotent rage when separation occurred. In Dr. Littner's words: "His history is typical of a person who is particularly sensitive to, and deeply troubled by, every aspect of growing up that implies independence. He seems to have been unable to deal adequately with such steps in maturation as going off to first grade and learning in school, or being able to use his intelligence to progress properly through school, or being able to retain a job or being able to manage a marital situation. He was unable to use the anxieties and mental tensions that accompany increasing independence, as a spur to further personality growth. Instead, he sought an outlet for the tensions through a variety of hysterical and other neurotic mechanisms. He has had many moves towards independence (he did try to get jobs; he did try a marriage) but he has never been able to tolerate them for very long."

It was not only Speck's inability to "mourn" over life's natural crises, including the death of his father when he was a boy (he told Dr. Littner the only thing he remembered about his father's death was standing and looking at the casket), but the experiences in his life, including violent episodes with an alcoholic, brutal stepfather, that caused Speck to commit the vicious murders.

One would guess, too, that somehow his mother unconsciously or consciously condoned his early displays of violence, so that he kept indulging in them. (Perhaps she unconsciously encouraged him to show a violence to the stepfather that she didn't dare but wished to.) His body was covered with scars from the knife fights of a lifetime and accidents that had occurred on motorcycles, in falls out of trees, crashes in cars and when driving a truck. He had been picked up by the police eight times since the age of thirteen for violent acts, and spent time in prison.

Dr. Hyman Spotnitz, who has treated and written about schizophrenia, concludes that if a mother encourages a child to express extreme violence and rage, the child may turn to crime in later life, having had her tacit approval to do so. Whereas if a mother punishes a child for expressing a show of anger, the child, if he has intense rage, may turn inward the murder he feels for her and become schizophrenic.[21]

Dr. Sandor Ferenczi suggested the possibility that children who received harsh treatment from their mothers, either physically or psychologically, may die easily and willingly. They fall ill, or live a cynical, unhappy, fearful life filled with guilt, depression and loneliness, killing themselves psychologically.[22]

Ferenczi said of a group of children not wanted by their parents, "All the indications show that these children had observed the conscious and unconscious signs of the aversion or impatience of the mother and their desire to live had been broken by it."

Dr. Sandor Lorand also established as an important factor in depression "the threatening, frustrating, punishing attitude of the mother."[23] He described a depressed woman who was "convinced that her mother was dangerous." Her mother "expressed disgust at the act of suckling babies," and told her many times that "mothers should never be born because they suffer so much."

We do know that parents abuse children physically. At least ten thousand children are beaten and seriously injured each year, according to the Children's Division of the American Humane Association. Physical assaults on children may be a more frequent cause of death than such well-recognized and thoroughly studied diseases as leukemia, cystic fibrosis, and muscular dystrophy, and may rank with automobile accidents, some authorities say.

Legislation to curb child abuse, practically unheard of before 1960, today is in effect in most states. These laws, chiefly intended to aid physicians in reporting child abuse cases, assure the physician immunity for a mistaken diagnosis. Physicians usually are reluctant to report such cases for fear the evidence will not stand up in court, and because of their own inability to believe parents could attack their own children.

The William Alanson White Institute, where emphasis is placed on the relationship between child and parents as the cause of emotional illness, has done studies showing that in a considerable number of cases, patients have been subjected to severe cruelty by a parent, but always the parent "wore a little mask to conceal the sheer brutality of what was going on."

Dr. Joseph Rheingold asks: "Why is man the only species whose behavior is so forcibly motivated by hate— by hostile protest and rebellion, by domination and exploitation, by recrimination, vindictiveness, and revenge? Why is homicide-suicide a basic potential of human life?" He answers: "It is because of the hurt inflicted upon the infant, the unbearable fact of human existence that the person who bestows life and upon whom the child is helplessly dependent also wishes to extinguish life and suppress its spontaneity."[24]

A number of analysts, in studying the need to suffer, emphasized the use of masochism as a child's way of trying to get love from parents who are cruel to him and unconsciously hate him. The very depressed person is seen as someone who, in childhood, was unloved or directly hated by his mother. This would explain the feeling of worthlessness and self-hate in depression. Some analysts regard the suffering in depression as an attempt on the part of the ego to pulverize itself in order to hold on to an idealized image of someone who is loved, who is necessary for its survival. In other words, masochism is the outgrowth of a non-loving relationship with the mother and the person, under the dominance of the masochistic pattern, gives up part of his ego in order to save the rest.

This means that children who are depressed suffer in order to survive. The child's response to the parent's hatred and his absorption of the parent's concealed wish to kill him may result in emotional illness, and may be an essential element in the formation of depression, suggests Dorothy Bloch.[25]

Her experience in treating children has led her to conclude, she says, that a child's survival appears to depend on the feeling of being loved by parents. "Unless it is recognized that the child must maintain the hope of being loved in order to live, then what follows when the feeling of being loved is missing and is supplanted by the feeling that the parents hate, and may have a concealed wish to destroy, to the child must seem forever mystifying," she says. She adds that a child tends to distort and misinterpret certain kinds of experiences and may interpret a parent's illness or death or absence as a sign of hate. But "a major source of his suffering may be his response to the feeling that the parents harbor a wish to destroy him."

The child deceives himself into believing that he is the cause of their hatred, feels worthless and thus continues to feed the hope "without which he cannot live," that "if he can change and become more worthy, he may still win their love. This delusion both sustains him and perpetuates his suffering." If at any point in his life the delusion is torn apart and the actual truth revealed, she adds, "that he himself had little to do with his parents' feelings, but that they did hate and want to destroy him—then all hope is lost and he may be in danger of committing suicide."

In other words, the depth of the hatred of the parent for the child determines the depth of the child's depression. For children inevitably accept the validity of their parent's feelings, as Miss Bloch points out:

They feel lovable where they experience love. Where they find hate and violently destructive feelings they invariably blame themselves and conclude that they deserve neither love nor life.

The first reactions a baby has are fear and rage. The rage is the origin of aggression—rage is the feeling, aggression is the act. Aggression in turn inspires fear and may be turned back on the self, rather than directed outward.

The mother is the baby's protector against danger and helplessness. If *she* proves to be a danger, he is irrevocably doomed. His fear of losing her, however, is even greater than his fear *of* her. At least she is *there*—her absence is the greatest of all dangers.

As Dr. Willi Hoffer put it:

Perhaps we should regard the interplay between self and object as the central paradox of emotional development: that the child needs his mother's love in order to be able to love himself, in order to be able to do without her love; then he should be able to love another person as he was loved by his mother.[26]

We all have to get over the belief in magic which we carry from childhood. The more painful the childhood, the more imperfect and hateful the parents, the greater the child's need for magic, because the weaker he feels up against the cruel giants. They may be cruel, yet they are all he has to love, and all he has to lose, and he will fight that loss with all his might. It is a hard psychic row for children to hoe, to realize that a parent can sometimes be unlovable and cruel, not always a god or goddess.

Even when we become emotionally mature (that goal of goals) the unconscious part of our mind will still hold some feeling of mourning for the lost pleasures of infancy. But if we are fairly realistic about life we will go on to find more appropriate pleasures, with a suitable substitute for our lost love.

6

〈×〉〈×〉〈×〉〈×〉〈×〉〈×〉〈×〉〈×〉〈×〉〈×〉〈×〉〈×〉〈×〉〈×〉〈×〉〈×〉〈×〉〈×〉

Special Light: The Creative Artist

The discovery that depression was accompanied by the
wish to make reparation, to re-create what in fantasy was
hated and destroyed, led to new speculations about the
nature of creativity. Not that creativity depends on depression, for it embodies far more, but that depression
somehow might be an unconscious force in the creative
process.

Not everyone sinks into apathy or retreats behind a
stone wall of uncommunication when depression strikes.
Our sad or morose moods need not necessarily be destructive. While gripped by such a mood, a man may
paint a work of art, compose a symphony, write a book
or make love. Moods have their magical qualities as well
as their earthbound ones.

As Swinburne wrote:

> *Many loves of many a mood and many a kind*
> *Fill the life of man and mould the secret mind.*

Every expression of productivity and creativity constitutes a conquest of death, says Dr. Joost A. M. Meerloo.[1]
In reverse, we might say that every expression of depression constitutes a giving in to death.

Instead of sinking into what Dr. Meerloo calls "the
deathly abyss of depression," the creative person turns his
depressive tendencies both to his and society's advantage.
He uses depression in its most constructive sense as he

seeks solitude rather than loneliness. The feeling of loneliness differs from solitude in that no psychic pain is felt
in the latter, while loneliness is associated with the anguish of depression. In solitude there is no alienation
from the self or others. The time alone is used to think
creatively or to enjoy the self. There is no loss of identity
but rather an enhancement of self.

Not that some creative people fail to be depressed. The
most creative people are sometimes among the most depressed. But they manage to pull themselves out of their
suffering long enough to create.

Possibly one of the most depressed writers who ever
lived was Dostoevski. He wrote in fiction form of many
of his inner conflicts, including the wish to murder *(Crime
and Punishment)* and the fanaticism of gambling *(The
Gambler)*. Gambling, when it cannot be controlled, is an
expression of the masochistic part of depression, the
seeking of pleasure through pain.

The famous sculptor, the late Alberto Giacometti, did
not try to hide his depression. He was known to his
friends as a man who possessed an attitude of "earnest
despair." His biographer, James Lord, asked if he ever
thought of suicide.

"Every day," he said.

He talked so often about killing himself that his wife,
Annette, once told him, "Do it or shut up." He replied he
would commit suicide, but only under one condition, that
he could come back to life and describe the sensation.

In the violence of his despair, at times he would smash
sculpture he had created even though he knew it would
bring him a high price. Even when he had money, he
continued to live and work in the cramped squalor of a
garret in one of the poorest sections of Paris.

Edgar Allan Poe is another whose life seemed to be a
series of depressions as he lost several women important
to him, starting with his own mother, who died when he
was a child. It would appear no accident that his stories
were full of the murder and violence he must have felt,
which were masked by the depression. His excessive
drinking was also a sign of deep depression.

Among those who achieved greatness but whose life showed deeply depressed moods was Abraham Lincoln. After the death of Ann Rutledge, he became incapacitated for months with melancholia. Again, in 1841 he fell into so deep a depression that he was suicidal. On the advice of doctors, friends watched him carefully, removing all knives and dangerous instruments from his presence. On the day of his wedding to Mary Todd, the guests appeared but Lincoln did not. He was found in his room, deep in dejection. He was quoted as saying he was the most unhappy man alive and that "if what I feel were equally distributed to the whole human family, there would not be one cheerful face on earth. Whether I shall ever be better, I cannot tell; I awfully forebode I shall not." His law partner described him as a "hopeless victim of melancholy." His wife's relatives thought him "insane."

The politician who achieves the greatness of a Lincoln, or the artist who becomes a Giacometti, manages to surmount his depressive feelings. He has the ability *in spite of his depression* to use his energy constructively. He has the strength to indulge in the highest form of what Freud called "sublimation." This is the psychic process of putting our sexual and aggressive energy into behavior that is of benefit to ourselves and society.

SEEDS OF CREATIVITY

What are the seeds of creativity? "We laymen have always wondered greatly—like the cardinal who put the question to Ariosto—how that strange being, the poet, comes by his material," said Freud. "What makes him able to carry us with him in such a way and to arouse emotions in us of which we thought ourselves perhaps not even capable?"[2]

If we ask the poets themselves, "they give us no explanation or at least no satisfactory explanation," Freud said. He added, "The knowledge that not even the clearest insight into the factors conditioning the choice of imaginative material, or into the nature of the ability to fashion that material, will ever make writers of us does not in any way detract from our interest."

Since it is the wish that lies at the heart of all fantasy, some actual experience which has made a strong impression on the writer stirs up memory of an earlier experience which then arouses a wish that finds fulfillment in the work in question, Freud held. In this work, elements of the recent event and the old memory "should be discernible."

A writer would give readers no pleasure if he disclosed his wishes directly, Freud said. He explained why this is so:

When we hear such phantasies they repel us, or at least leave us cold. But when a man of literary talent presents his plays, or relates what we take to be his personal daydreams, we experience great pleasure arising probably from many sources. How the writer accomplishes this is his innermost secret; the essential *ars poetica* lies in the technique by which our feeling of repulsion is overcome, and this has certainly to do with those barriers erected between every individual being and all others. We can guess at two methods used in this technique. The writer softens the egotistical character of the day-dream by changes and disguises, and he bribes us by the offer of a purely formed, that is, aesthetic pleasure in the presentation of his phantasies. The increment of pleasure which is offered us in order to release yet greater pleasure arising from deeper sources in the mind is called an "incitement premium" or technically "fore-pleasure." I am of the opinion that all the aesthetic pleasure we gain from the works of imaginative writers is of the same type as this "fore-pleasure," and that the true enjoyment of literature proceeds from the release of tensions in our minds. Perhaps much that brings about this result consists in the writer's putting us into a position in which we can enjoy our own day-dreams without reproach or shame.

In other words, although all of us have the same powerful unconscious drives, the artist has the ability to express them aesthetically. He is not overwhelmed by his anger, fear or depression. The artist represses, as we all do. But he is able to use his repressions to build beauty. He, like everyone, experiences what Freud called "the return of the repressed," but with the purpose of glorifying life, not giving in to his conflicts.

Freud suggested that the artist was a person of "special gifts" who had a "flexibility of repressions." This "flexibility" allowed the artist to project his inner turmoil on the stage of his production so that an audience could witness and take part in the artistic experience. The flexibility also allowed the energy bound up in repression to be freed. This energy could then be used to transform unconscious fantasies into conscious works of art.

Freud wrote that

the artist is originally a man who turns from reality because he cannot come to terms with the demand for renunciations of instinctual satisfaction as it is first made, and who then in fantasy life allows full play to his erotic and ambitious wishes. But he finds a way of return from this world of fantasy back to reality; with his special gifts he moulds his fantasies into a new kind of reality; and men concede them a justification as valuable reflections of actual life.[3]

Freud said, further, that the artist

turns away from reality and transfers all his interest, and all his libido too, on to the creation of his wishes in the life of fantasy, from which the way might readily lead to neurosis. There must be many factors in combination to prevent this becoming the whole outcome of his development; it is well known how often artists in particular suffer from partial inhibition of their capacities through neurosis. Probably their constitution is endowed with a powerful capacity for sublimation and with a certain flexibility in the repressions determining the conflict.[4]

Freud held that behind all artistic and worthwhile endeavors lay the sexual urge, sublimated. "Our most highly valued cultural heritage has been acquired at the cost of sexuality and by the restriction of sexual motive forces," he said. The ability of a person to sublimate his primitive, savage instincts plays an important part in the success of any personal psychoanalysis "and the same is true of his capacity for rising superior to the crude life of the instincts."

Freud defined sublimation as the psychic process "through which the powerful excitations from individual sources of sexuality are discharged and utilized in other spheres so that a considerable increase of psychic capacity results from an, in itself, dangerous, predisposition."[5]

This increase of psychic capacity forms one of the sources of artistic activity, Freud said. According to whether such sublimation is complete or incomplete, "the analysis of the character of highly gifted, especially of artistically disposed persons, will show any proportionate blending between productive ability, perversion, and neurosis."

Psychoanalysts agree in a general sense that creativity is a successful sublimation of strong, primitive drives. It is a defense made in an attempt to solve emotional conflicts. These conflicts, inevitable ones, arise as infantile, instinctual drives clash with the demands of society.

To put it into a poet's words, as Coleridge wrote: "To carry on the feelings of childhood into the powers of manhood, that is the character and privilege of genius."

Or as Rilke said in *Letters to a Young Poet,* giving instruction on how to create: "I could give you no advice but this: to go into yourself, and to explore the depths whence your life wells forth."

The choice of the specific sublimation, such as creativity, depends on what Freud called "over-determination." This implies the impact of many psychic experiences in the childhood of each life. He gave a dramatic example of such sublimation in his classic study of Leonardo da Vinci.[6] This book about da Vinci is also noted for its contribution to the understanding of homosexuality, and for its eloquent description of the importance of a mother's sexual attitude toward her infant, as far as his later psychosexual development goes.

Da Vinci, as a boy between the ages of three and five,

was torn away by his wealthy father from his mother, Caterina, whom his father never married—she was a peasant girl who later married someone else. The only definite information about Leonardo's childhood, according to Freud, is furnished in a Florentine tax register from the year 1457 in which Vinci Leonardo is mentioned among the members of the family as a five-year-old illegitimate child of Ser Piero da Vinci. His father thereafter remained childless, and the boy was brought up by his father and Donna Albieri, "a loving stepmother," Freud said. Leonardo did not leave their house until he entered the studio of Andrea del Verrocchio as an apprentice, at an unknown age.

Freud theorized that the smile on the face of the Mona Lisa reflected a memory of Leonardo's real mother in the first years of his childhood, a woman forced to give up her son to her most aristocratic rival, as she had once before given up her lover. (We can imagine the despair in a little boy of three or four, seized from his mother's arms forever.)

Following the appearance of the Mona Lisa, artists in Italy depicted in madonnas and prominent ladies the humble dipping of the head and the peculiar blissful smile of the Mona Lisa, modeled after the poor peasant girl, Caterina, who brought to the world a noble son destined "to paint, investigate and suffer," according to Freud. Leonardo succeeded in reproducing in the face of the Mona Lisa "the double sense comprised in the smile, namely, the promise of unlimited tenderness and sinister threat," Freud held.

Why the "sinister threat"? Freud explained that he based this interpretation on the only childhood memory about which Leonardo ever wrote, the one time he interspersed in his scientific statements "a communication from his childhood." In describing scientifically how a vulture flies, Leonardo suddenly became personal. He wrote:

It seems that it had been destined before that I should occupy myself so thoroughly with the vulture, for it comes to my mind as a very early memory, when I was still in the cradle, a vulture came down to me, opened my mouth with his tail and struck me many times with his tail against my lips.

Freud interpreted this as a fantasy which Leonardo formed in later years but which applied to his childhood. Such a memory concealed "invaluable evidences" of the most important features of Leonardo's psychic development, Freud said, and he ventured the attempt to fill the gaps in the history of Leonardo's early life through the analysis of this infantile fantasy.

Freud's interpretation:

The love of the mother became his destiny; it determined his fate and the privations which were in store for him. The impetuosity of the caressing to which the vulture phantasy points was only too natural. The poor forsaken mother had to give vent through mother's love to all her memories of love enjoyed as well as to all her yearnings for more affection; she was forced to it, not only in order to compensate herself for not having a husband, but also the child for not having a father to love it. In the manner of all ungratified mothers she thus took her little son in place of her husband, and robbed him of a part of his virility by maturing too early his erotic life. The love of the mother for the suckling whom she nourishes and cares for is something far deeper-reaching than her later affection for the growing child. It is of the nature of a fully gratified love affair, which fulfills not only all the psychic wishes but also all physical needs, and when it represents one of the forms of happiness attainable by man, it is due, in no little measure, to the possibility of gratifying without reproach also wish feelings which were long repressed and designated as perverse.

Freud added that even in the happiest young married life, the father feels that his child, especially the little boy, has become his rival and this causes an antagonism against the favorite son which is deeply rooted in the unconscious.

Freud stated in this book, as he had before many times, that "in the first three or four years of life impressions become fixed and modes of reactions are formed toward the outer world which can never be robbed of their importance by any later experiences." He also said that "it seems that childhood is not that blissful idyl into which we later distort it, that, on the contrary, children are lashed through the years of childhood by the wish to become big, and to imitate the grown-ups." (If this wish becomes too intense, the child will most certainly be depressed because of the impossible odds against his competing successfully with his parents.)

When, in the prime of his life, Leonardo reencountered "that blissful and ecstatic smile as it had once encircled his mother's mouth in caressing," he had long been under the ban of an inhibition, forbidding him ever again to desire such tenderness from women's lips, Freud said. Leonardo endeavored, however, as an artist, to reproduce this smile with his brush. It appeared in most of his pictures, whether he painted them himself or they were created by his pupils under his direction.

The "familiar, fascinating smile," according to Freud, "leads us to infer that it is a love secret." He surmised it was possible that, in his works, Leonardo "disavowed and artistically conquered the unhappiness of his love life, in that he represented the wish fulfillment of the boy infatuated with his mother in such blissful union of the male and female nature."

Leonardo was accused, tried and acquitted of homosexuality. Of this Freud said that, in Leonardo's unconscious, he was still tied to his mother, as he had been in childhood, by erotically tinged feelings that were so strong they constituted the only personal comment he ever put in his diary. It was a comment that "came to the knowledge of posterity as something incomprehensible."

His mother and his pupils (the supposed targets of his homosexuality) were his sexual objects, as far as the sexual repression dominating his nature would allow him to express them. The appearance of the homosexual situation in the vulture fantasy (Freud compares the memory of the vulture sticking its tail into the baby's mouth with the homosexual act, equating tail with penis) becomes comprehensible, Freud concluded, when the interpretation is made: "Through the erotic relations to my mother I became a homosexual."

The absence of a man from the home during Leonardo's early life was another factor contributing to the development of homosexuality. Freud said he was impressed by the number of cases of homosexuality in which the father had been absent from the start of the child's life or disappeared early in it, "so that the boy was altogether under feminine influence."

Leonardo also must have been tortured by "the great questions" of childhood, such as where children come from, and what the father has to do with their origin, Freud maintained.

When creative curiosity is highly developed, as it was with Leonardo, whose investigations took him into almost all realms of science (in every one of which he was a discoverer or, at least, a prophet), it is likely, Freud explained, that two other expectations will be verified. It is probable the very forcible impulse of creative curiosity was already active in earliest childhood and "its supreme sway" fixed by infantile impressions. Also, that originally the impulse to look creatively at life "drew upon sexual motive powers for its reinforcement, so that it later can take the place of a part of the sexual life."

Such a person, said Freud, would then "investigate with that passionate devotion which another would give to his love, and he could investigate instead of loving." He added, "We would venture the conclusion of a sexual reinforcement not only in the impulse to investigate, but also in most other cases of special intensity of an impulse."

THE ARTIST: "TRIUMPH OVER AGGRESSION"

Freud in his later years attributed to the aggressive instinct a power equal to the sexual, so that the aggressive or hostile urge was seen as present in sublimation, along with the sexual urge. Ella Sharpe, British psychoanalyst, talks of art as "the need to know . . . heightened by aggressive phantasy." She calls knowledge of reality "a bulwark against phantasy." (And creativity is one way of knowing things.)[7]

"Art . . . is a sublimation rooted in the primal identification with the parents . . . a magical incorporation," she says. "The artist is able to put the hostility inherent in incorporation (a psychic swallowing of the parent) into a work of art in which he can control, in an external form, an introjected image or images. His creativity is a way of achieving mastery over his fantasies, and over such psychic processes as compression, symbolization, identification, projection, and restitution."

In other words, the artist is "recreating symbolically the very image that hostility has destroyed," she says. The artist is able to "triumph over aggression." He has enough of the "good mother," the "good imago," in him, to want to create, not destroy, even though he may feel destructive. The artist "creates pictures with the symbolical substances which, when disordered and unrhythmical, mean for the unconscious mind menace and destruction."

The child persists in the artist; art as sublimation arises from the stage of infancy before speech is acquired, she holds.

The arts communicate emotional experience which is dynamically in touch with emotions that the child could not express in words. The child communicated it by crooning, gurgling, crying, screaming, by gesture, urinating, defaecating. The artist, the "pure" artist, communicates his emotional experience by manipulation of sound, gesture, water, paint, words. The same bodily powers are used as in babyhood but infinitely developed, the same substances, symbolically (as in water and oils), are used; but with one immense difference, namely, the submission of these to extraordinary control and manipulation, but a control that is an utilization of these same things to the end of a creation of harmony and design.

By "pure" art, Miss Sharpe means "those products of creative genius which have been dictated only by the inner laws and urges of the creator." The artist "can be nothing else but an artist," a man who would pursue his unconsciously determined goal "to the verge of starvation."

The artist creates everything through a sensuous contact, "yet the greater the artist, the more does his work become objective, freed from personal partial bias, and exhibit universal truth." Hamlet may be, in essence, the story of Shakespeare, but it is also the story of all men, she points out.

It is the urge to make reparation, which is part of the depressive position, once felt for the mother, later transferred to new objects, that drives an artist, in part, according to Melanie Klein.[8] As he grows, an infant turns his interest from its first object, his mother's breast, to other objects which become a substitute for the breast. It is while he suffers the anxieties attendant on "the depressive position" during the end of the first year of his life that he learns to relate to the world by projection, deflection and other psychic processes "and distributes desires and emotions, as well as guilt and the urge to make reparation on to new objects and interests," Mrs. Klein puts it.

Intending to write an article on sublimation just before she died, the late Dr. Minna Emch, Chicago psychoanalyst, left notes applicable to depression and to the understanding of the creative mind.

She thought the psychoanalytic concept of sublimation an unnecessary hypothesis. She quoted one of the definitions of sublimation (from the Oxford English Dictionary, Vol. 2): "To raise to an elevated sphere or exalted state; to make (especially morally or spiritually) sublime." She also quoted a line from Macaulay: "His very selfishness therefore is sublimed into public spirit."

She said she thought that sublimation was a term "contaminated by ethics, culture and morality," in that what might be considered healthy sublimation for some was not for others. She pointed out that acceptable sublimation in one culture differed from that in another. She objected to the concept as representing "one of the few of Freud's Puritan tendencies which he allowed to get into psychoanalytic theory." She held it introduced "non-analytic judgment values."

Dr. Emch thought of sublimation not as a concept standing by itself but as the end result of a series of psychic processes that started when an infant tried to achieve what psychoanalysts call "homeostasis." This is a balance within the individual, which he tries to keep by discharging tension as best he can.

She described creativity and all sublimation "as the result" in a continuum from early narcissism, when the world revolves around the self, to the acceptance of the aims of reality. Creativity, particularly, occurred when, in response to intense emotions, "exaltation" was the mood in infancy, rather than depression, she maintained.

For instance, a baby feels anxiety, perhaps because his mother has not fed him enough. He is angry, wants to bite her breast, maybe even does. If she is a troubled person, she may push him away, an angry expression on her face, or slap him, or yell at him. He realizes that to get her love, to ensure further feeding, he cannot bite her even though he feels angry. He learns to repress anger, to feel guilty, then depressed. What is called reaction formation, or reversal, may set in (the showing of the opposite emotion—compliance instead of rebellion) as he realizes he must accept the reality that he cannot bite his mother when he feels enraged.

Many ways are open to him to appease his overwhelming anger. He may fall sick, thus begging her for pity, demanding she take care of him so he will live (he may even die if he is angry enough). Or he can use his fantasies to dream of eating her up. Or he can think of imaginary food. Or he may refuse to reason at all and become mentally retarded or psychotic.

His ability to use his fantasies creatively depends on the strength of his slowly growing ego, depends on how early and how deep the emotional damage, how severe the wounds to his narcissism. If those wounds are not too deep (we all are wounded somewhat by the weaning process—Freud said that "for however long a child is fed at his mother's breast he will always be left with a conviction after he is weaned that his feeding was too short and too little") the infant, in Dr. Emch's words, can "replenish the narcissism, which then leads to the modification of reality via channels of interpersonal relationship or meaningful communication." One of the forms of the latter is creativity.

"The creative phenomena of genius can be related to intensity of effort and tremendous concentration of emotion in a particular area," said Dr. Emch. Such intensity and concentration starts in infancy, psychoanalysts agree. Carrying Dr. Emch's theory one step further, we can see that a baby who may be overly aroused sexually by his own erotic impulses, or overstimulated sexually by parents or a nurse or relatives, may try to handle these feelings of tension in one of several ways. He may scream in rage. Or wet his bed. Or hit his head against the side of the crib. Or refuse to eat or to sleep. Or overeat or oversleep.

After a while he learns to repress some of his emotions when they bring anger from his parents, and his fantasies come into play as one way to hold down the repression.

Psychoanalytic knowledge provides us with a rational method for determining the origins of the thoughts of the creative writer, says Dr. John W. Markson.[9] Fantasies which originate in the unconscious and are secondarily "elaborated, re-worded and polished with linguistic skill can be considered to be *written-out*," he explains. The result of the "written-out" primary process becomes interpretable in both its open and its hidden content. The original thought or idea may be painful and thus is comparable to a symptom; it may help to reveal a conflict, as a symptom does, which is "threatening the emotional integrity of the author and is attenuated by writing."

"LOVE AFFAIR WITH THE WORLD"

The creative spirit has been described in detail by Dr. Phyllis Greenacre.[10] Creative people are not immune from neurosis and psychosis but neither is there an "intrinsic connection," she says. To her, creativity is a special capacity which may or may not be associated with great ability. It does not seem to have a great deal to do with superior intelligence, even though intelligence may contribute to the productions of the creative person.

She declares there are two main questions: Is creative talent inborn? What are the basic characteristics of creative talent?

She knows of no decisive study to support that it is inherited. It is difficult, if not impossible, to tell potentially talented infants from less gifted ones. She concludes that not heredity, but identification with the parents is important; identification may simulate inheritance—it may appear as though neurosis, for instance, was inherited "when scrutiny shows it is passed on by contact, direct and indirect, through subtle processes of identification."

Dr. Greenacre says that she herself is "largely convinced that genius is a 'gift of the Gods' and is already laid down at birth, probably as a sport development [a variation from the normal] which finds especially favorable soil for its evolution in families where there is also a good inheritance of intellect and a favorable background for identification."

She speaks of "the love affair with the world which seems to be an obligatory condition in the development of great talent or genius." (Similar to Dr. Emch's factor of "exaltation.") She maintains that "from the study of lives of artists and from such analytic experience as I have had with them, it seems that the artist invariably has some kind of genuine love affair." Such love affairs with the world are sometimes conducted at the expense of the individual, she adds.

She calls writing "an act of love." She says, "The

artistic product has rather universally the character of a love gift, to be brought as near perfection as possible and to be presented with pride and misgiving."

A critical situation in infancy may cause creativity, she believes. For instance, a gifted child, forced to exert control of his bowels, may more readily and extensively than other children play with mud or clay as fecal substitutes, which he begins to fashion according to his imaginative wishes.

Dr. Greenacre also says that "skill in a gifted individual is but part of the unfolding of the imagination which may originally gain impetus in connection with masturbatory activity but becomes liberated from it."

Oedipal wishes are apparently desexualized from genital aims, but not renounced, she holds. "It seems that the gifted children may solve their Oedipal problems less decisively than the more average children do." (This might well follow, because they are more sensitive to the parents' needs and wishes and likely to remain more attached to them.)

Declaring that "the experience of awe in childhood" is described with special intensity by creatively gifted persons, she speculates that there may be an early image of the godlike father, a "penis awe." Possibly there was actual seeing of the adult tumescent penis at a time when the child was in a particularly sensitive state, which gives rise to sensations of invigoration, inspiration and awe, a "near ecstasy in one's own body state," an "inner explosiveness."

Dr. Greenacre also suggests that the infancy of the gifted person or genius holds an early and marked sensitivity to sensory stimulation from the mother's breast. She writes, "We might conceive that the potentially gifted infant would react to the mother's breast with an intensity of the impression of warmth, smell, moisture, the feel of the texture of the skin and the vision of the roundness of the form."

Recalling Freud's observation that the most gifted children early in life show a curiosity about things sexual, Dr. Daniel E. Schneider makes the point that it is as though particularly gifted men identify themselves not solely with the mother and father but with all the wider excursions of relationships—with the "unseen" act [of sexual intercourse], the "unfelt" pleasure and the "unforeseen but inevitable" result of sexual creativity . . . It is in brief the riddle of the Sphinx solved at its highest level. It is as though the child identifies with father, mother *and* the "unseen, unfelt but inevitable" act and process of creation.[11]

The sensually stimulated baby is apt to be the angry baby, for at that stage of life the sexual and aggressive drives are closely intertwined. As a child grows up, if he is given constructive outlets by his parents, he is often able to divert his powerful emotions, and the fantasies woven around them, into creative channels. (In contrast, sensually stimulated babies whose parents fail to give them constructive outlets may turn into schizophrenics, murderers, suicides.)

This might explain why the sexual lives of so many of our gifted people go awry. In one sense, the early sexual precocity may have driven them to creativity but also to premature heightened sexual arousal, so they were unable to move ahead to adult sexuality. The creative person who is also a homosexual, or an alcoholic, or who kills himself, is showing the existence of those early powerful sexual and aggressive urges, so intense they spill over not only into his creative spirit but into other parts of his life.

As Mrs. Klein pointed out, every physical impulse or urge has as its psychic counterpart a fantasy or fantasies. Fantasies from both the oral and anal stages of early life are part of the artist's emotional equipment. After all, the first production of life is feces and one of the unconscious motives of the artist may be to master that first productive process. Or to keep producing for mother so she will continue to love him.

From the oral stage, the artist may have unconscious fantasies about biting or devouring his mother and then making reparation in kind as he later creates something for her to devour aesthetically. Or he may be providing himself with something to devour with his eyes, or ears, or other senses. Artistic productions, too, may be symbolic substitutes for babies (little boys unconsciously want to be able to have babies). Or they may symbolize the penis, which is power, true creative power.

The creative person takes his imaginative, wild fantasies and forms them into images of loveliness, of eloquence, of communication. He harnesses inner chaos and depression so he is able to produce works that add to the meaning of his life and the world's understanding of man. He "sees things in a manner peculiar to himself. He then gives his vision the form forced upon him by his underlying personality," as Emanuel F. Hammer says.[12]

One reason we honor and exalt the artist is because we all know how difficult it is for man to sublimate his savage drives creatively. It is a great achievement to channel mad fantasy into sane forms of beauty. To allow fantasies to plunge us into depression is the easy way. To turn them to enhancing the world, to bring joy to our fellowman, is the hard way. A cliché has it that it is just as easy to be happy as sad, but that is not true. It is very hard to be happy for many.

PSYCHOANALYSIS DOES *NOT* KILL CREATIVITY

Artists who have been psychoanalyzed do not lose their creativity, but their depression. The psychoanalyst helps them to lift repressions, not so their creativity will be in any way lessened, but so they may live as far less anguished human beings.

Depression may be a consequence of someone *not* being able to create. He will have less reason to be depressed if whatever conflicts blocking his ability to create are eased.

The analyst helps the artist overcome depression. As Dr. Lawrence S. Kubie says, "No one need fear that getting well will cause an atrophy of his creative drive. . . . This illusory fear rests on the erroneous assumption that it is that which is unconscious in us which makes us creative, whereas in fact the unconscious is our straitjacket, rendering us as stereotyped and as sterile and as repetitive as the neurosis itself." The goal in analysis, he explains, is to seek to free preconscious processes from "the distortions and obstructions interposed by unconscious processes and from the pedestrian limitations of conscious processes. The unconscious can spur it on. The conscious can criticize and correct and evaluate. But creativity is a product of preconscious activity. This is the challenge."[13]

Perhaps many a successful artist might have saved himself from gripping depression had he gone into analysis. For there are some to whom success brings depression, then destruction. Just as they achieve what they have always wanted, they must destroy themselves, not understanding why success has not brought them release from their devastating depression.

There is a "creative depression" or "depression of the artist" that is part of the cycle of creativity, Erika Freeman said, in a special interview. It is connected with the building cycle that precedes the experience of the artistic creation, which is a form of birth. The depression following creation may be similar to that of the postpartum depression, she maintains. The artist is left with a sense of emptiness and helplessness, of castration and the conviction he will never be able to create again.

She believes the artist has "excessive energy, brilliantly sublimated." In some way he has received special nourishment from his mother. She quotes Freud as saying that the favored son of a mother must be a success.

The depression that follows success has caused a number of writers, painters and actors to kill themselves as they reach the pinnacle of fame. Some do so outright in suicide. Others kill themselves slowly, with alcohol or pills. Or they are the victims of accidents which they unconsciously seek. Or they go insane, as Nijinsky did.

Consciously, such artists feel a despair and emptiness and disappointment so great they cannot bear to go on living. But unconsciously, success has precipitated physical or psychological suicide because, in part, it symbolizes the fulfillment of the forbidden Oedipal wish—they are successful in beating out mama (or papa) and getting daddy (or mama) at long last and then must punish themselves for violating the dreaded taboo of incest, which includes the unconscious murder of the parent of the opposite sex. On still an earlier level, as infants, "success" may also mean the murder of the mother who frustrated them and whom they occasionally wished dead.

One writer had a successful autobiography published in which, however, he spoke rather unsympathetically of his mother. Two months after the book appeared, she died. He felt what he had said about her in the book had killed her. He became so depressed he went into analysis. There he found that his book had nothing to do with her death, but that, as a child, he had unconsciously wished her dead at times because he felt she had frustrated him.

One of the reasons for disappointment in the creator after the appearance of a successful book or work of art may be that it has failed to provide the ample feeding (emotionally speaking) still being demanded of his mother by the childlike part of the artist.

In contrast to those who gain success and then cannot bear it are those with artistic potential who are so afraid of success they will not even make a stab at it. They cannot stand losing and they cannot stand winning. They waste their lives in halfhearted jabs at creating, belittling themselves and, often, others. We can but assume that somehow they lacked a strength in childhood that comes from feeling a certain amount of love and security, which would enable them to use their potential. They are still gripped too powerfully by the depression of infancy.

The ability to be creative is apparently the result of a number of things in the life of a man. For one, he must possess what Freud called "the special gifts" of the creative man—perhaps this is chiefly a sensitivity in infancy to a mother who is also sensitive.

The gifted person also has the strength to put into art

form some of the strong sexual and aggressive emotions that possess him. The artist as a young man and as a child has to receive enough love and approval so he is able to use his powerful feelings in creative, rather than destructive, manner. In some way, his mother and father make known to him that he is loved for what he produces. He will keep on producing more and more to keep their love. If a child feels little love, he may not try to use his energy to create because he will need most of it to keep hatred hidden.

The love and approval the artist receives as a child gives the nod to narcissistic expression. He feels he is entitled to an awareness of his own uniqueness. He can turn his natural exhibitionism outward, rebel with a cause, and share an experience, no matter how painful or embarrassing, with the world.

The artist also has the ability to discipline himself, at least enough to create (if not to stop drinking or being promiscuous). He puts his natural masochism to good use. As Tolstoi said, "One leaves a piece of one's own flesh in the inkpot each time one dips one's pen."

The artist also is carrying out both the conscious and unconscious wishes of his parents. He responds not only to what he hears them approve of (as in the case of Stanislavski, about whose life Dr. Philip Weissman has written) [14] but to what he *senses* they wish him to do.

There is also, as Dr. Emch put it, a sense of "exaltation" in his infancy, rather than defeatism. The artist has a courage that enables him to master much of his psychic pain. In a sense, creativity may be thought of as one way of fighting the depression that ensues naturally as a result of the inevitable rages of childhood which spring up in all of us.

Thus creativity serves as an attempt on the part of the very sensitive person to surmount the power of his destructive fantasies so they will not destroy himself or others. The artist is engaged first and foremost in a struggle with his primitive self. It is a struggle he wins, often to his own benefit, always to the benefit of mankind.

7

The Other Side: On Elation,
Humor and Laughter

Psychoanalysts have not given as much study to the other side of the coin—elation, or mania—as they have to depression. "The cheerful do not as a rule come for treatment," as Dr. Bertram D. Lewin says.[1]

In general, the "morbid happy states" have been taken pretty much as part of a circular picture, or as the outcome of a depressive process, Dr. Lewin points out. For analysts, the problem seemed solved once the causes of depression were understood. But, he says, all depressions are not accompanied by elation and many elations themselves occur or recur without an apparent depression.

When we feel elated, we are "in high spirits, proud and happy, joyful," according to Webster. We look on ourselves and the world with a benign, friendly eye. Feeling quarrelsome or aggressive or depressed is the thought furthest from our minds.

As with the depressed feeling, the elated feeling, when temperate, is a natural one. It is normal to be elated when something enjoyable or pleasurable happens. You feel exuberant when you fall in love, or get married, or discover you are going to have a baby, or achieve sudden success in a career, or hear good news about someone you love.

But there may be elation at inappropriate times, or all the time. In such cases, the person is using it to mask an underlying depression. Someone who laughs at his par-

ent's funeral, or at the breakup of his marriage, or at
news of a friend's bad luck, is showing improper use of
elation, as is the person who laughs at everything that
happens, whether sad or happy.

According to Dr. Lewin, elation is a "narcissistic neurosis like depression." It has its roots in the reactions of
early childhood, just as depression does.

But in elation, the underlying depression is denied.
Denial is used as defense as the person accepts only what
seems pleasurable. He rejects the unpleasant, including
any criticism of himself.

Denial may operate in a dual capacity, Dr. Lewin
declares. It may oppose the intellectual recognition of an
external fact such as the death of someone who was
loved. The elated person may believe the death did not
occur. Or denial may be used to oppose the emotional
impact of a realistic fact. Although admitting the death of
a loved one did occur, the person says, "Well, I really
don't care. It doesn't matter to me."

"In the elations we shall find that it is chiefly this
aspect of denial—the denial of the emotional impact of
reality—which influences the clinical picture," Dr. Lewin
says.

The effect of denial is "to rupture the intellectual rap-
port or emotional attuning of the ego with its environment." Dr. Lewin quotes Freud as stating that denials
are, for the most part, half measures, incomplete detach-
ments from reality. There is rejection, but there also is
some acceptance; these two contrary attitudes produce a
split in the ego.

Just as dreams represent fantasy that is "taken away
and split off from the ego's complete control and from
everyday influences," elation "splits off a fact-denying
part of the ego from the rest," he says.

The manic attack is a denial "of just such precipitating
situations as we have come, in psychoanalysis, to regard
as revivers of childhood conflicts and frustrations. A manic's flighty, dispersed attention to the environment fills his
consciousness and excludes or crowds into a corner facts
and topics that would trouble him or pain him."

Dr. Lewin does not believe mania is an escape from depression but that it represents a different defense from depression. Elation interrupts but does not terminate depression. The elation "puts aside the depression, which comes to light again later."

He believes that mania may be compared to sleep, in which reality is shut out, if we take into account that "dreams of different degrees of complexity and with a variable amount of censorship are also parts of sleep as we know it."

"Mania thus could be a kind of sleep even if it is not a deep sopor," Dr. Lewin says. "So considered, a typical elation or mania is seen to resemble the dream of a small child, with its playful fantasy wish fulfillments."

Dreams with a manifest (evident) elated mood, which contain laughter or appear to be "happy dreams," mean the reverse of what they appear to say, he maintains. The elation in such dreams is like manic elation, which denies reality.

Elation repeats the feeling of the baby at the breast after being fed. It is "a development of this primal sleep— the wish-fulfilling, dreaming sleep of a somewhat older child; it is a substitute sleep, or a sleep equivalent, guarded by a type of censorship that is created particularly to employ the defense mechanism, denial, and to prevent emotional acceptance [of a loss]."

Dr. Lewin points out that the midday nap, for instance, is a vestige of a childhood habit, connected with the infantile sleep after meals that started with the nursing situation.

A feeling of joyousness that is almost manic may follow normal mourning. Mourning may end in a heightened sense of well-being, increased sexual potency and capacity for work, and sublimation. Geza Roheim, anthropologist and psychoanalyst, reported that in certain primitive societies, the period of mourning a death was followed by a mammoth celebration.

We all know the feeling of a moderate amount of elation, of excitement and exuberance during which we have the sensation of being up on cloud nine. At such times we laugh easily, freely. We see life in humorous vein rather than taking it too seriously, as we do when we feel moody. Freud explained technically what happens thus to our psyche in his paper on "Humour" written in 1927. He said, "The grandeur of humour lies in the triumph of narcissism—the victorious assertion of the ego's invulnerability. The ego refuses to be disturbed by the provocations of reality and let itself be compelled to suffer."[2]

Humor is a normal escape from pain. It is a way of allowing some of our most unpleasurable emotions to come to the surface but in controlled fashion. Freud relates humor to the partial awareness of reality we have in childhood. He suggests humor is the ego's identification with childlike uncertainty plus the super-ego's "benevolent toleration" of this childhood uncertainty. The super-ego in depression he describes as "a kind of gathering-place for the death-instincts."

Dr. Walter A. Stewart, who has written on elation, says:

The most essential quality of the "humorous mode" is a toleration of the painful narcissistic injuries of childhood. Both jokes and humor turn an expected pain or anxiety into a playful feeling. Where the ego expects anger, pain, intellectual concern, tenderness, anxiety or pity, the situation turns out not to require these, and the ego is relieved to find that it can be unconcerned. Laughter is the result of relief from this expectation of concern, pain or anxiety.

Humor is "an alternative to depression." According to Dr. Stewart, it is basically

a non-psychotic method of the denial of reality. It manages to recapture the sense of what is pleasurable over the normal demands on the ego, which is required to deal not with what is pleasurable but what is real, even if it is painful. Humor tends to re-establish the judgment of good from bad as opposed to our usual demand to distinguish true from false.

But elation, he points out, when it is extreme depends on the pathological use of denying the truth to override the demands of reality.

In neurotic depression the person begs for love or demands love with the feeling of being unlovable. He reproaches both himself and the one from whom he seeks love for the lack of love. In contrast, the manic person who also demands love feels he is loved and loving. His love and aggression are turned in large part outward.

Psychiatric depression, according to Dr. Stewart, is more involved with aggression and fear of damaging the object. Mania is a further regression in which "no matter how greedy the person is, he does not destroy the breast if it is good, and is willing to destroy it if it is bad, because he feels he can always get another. It recalls the joke, 'You can eat your brother, 'Cause you can get another; But you mustn't eat your mother, Because you'll never get another.' " In mania, aggression is denied. Both the love and aggression are acted out, not turned inward as in depression.

In extreme depression, and in extreme elation, there is regression to the point where the person has little capacity to integrate the "good" and "bad" qualities in the self or the loved one. ("Regression" is a return to an earlier level of satisfaction or frustration. It is as though we say to ourselves, "This problem I am facing is too tough. I'm going back to an earlier one. Maybe I didn't solve that either, but it seems less difficult than what faces me now.") All that is "good" is taken in, all that is "bad" is blamed on the outside.

Or the reverse may exist, as Melanie Klein has pointed out. All the "bad" is now in the self, all the "good" on the outside. (There is fear of destroying the object and the chance of being loved, and instead the self is thought of as "bad" as a way of avoiding aggression.)

The fluctuation between depressive and manic feelings in infancy is an essential part of normal development, according to Mrs. Klein. She explained that when the depressive position of the last six months of the first year of life occurs, the ego is forced (in addition to earlier defenses) to develop other methods of defense against "pining" for the loved one. These defenses are fundamental to the organization of the ego. She called some of these methods "manic defenses" or "the manic position" because of their similarity to the manic moods seen in some adults.

The trouble with intense elation is that what goes up so far must come down, usually with a crash. Following the elation, there is emptiness and loneliness. For, when extreme, elation is based not on true enjoyment but is a defense against inner depression.

AGGRESSION WITHOUT GUILT

The emotion of elation, as the result of pleasure in laughter, may be a good deterrent to depression. We all esteem the one who is able to laugh, particularly at himself, as well as the one who gives us the chance to laugh (it is no wonder entertainers are paid far higher than teachers).

A laugh a day, if it is a genuine one, keeps depression away. Because through laughter, we release our aggression in a way at which we need feel no guilt, no depression. Temporarily, a repression is lifted, the energy tied up in the guilt and depression is freed and our spirit soars.

If we can laugh at what frightens or depresses us, we feel happier. Anything sacred made profane is funny. It should be no surprise that the butt of much wit centers on two wishes that are, to many of us, the most dangerous— our wish to kill and our wish to be more sexually free. Sometimes both are combined in one joke.

We have learned to laugh at any taboo—even incest. Recently Frank Sinatra, while appearing at the Fontainebleau in Miami, asked the audience, "Did it ever occur to you that the Governor of Alabama is a mother?" The audience roared. Then Sinatra said, "I could add another word to that one but I won't because that's how I feel about her husband, not her," and the audience laughed even louder.

A less direct joke about incest made the rounds several years ago. A Jewish mother talking to her neighbor says proudly, "Mine son has just started seeing a psychiatrist."

"What's wrong with him?" asks the neighbor.

"The doctor says he is sick from something called Oedipus," says the mother worriedly.

"Oedipus-Schmedipus!" scoffs her friend. "As long as he loves his mother."

By what a man laughs at, you may know him. The man who compulsively tells dirty jokes to the exclusion of all others is likely to be a sexually inhibited man, tied to the anal pleasure of early development. On the other hand, if a man cannot laugh at an off-color joke which is nevertheless clever, he is probably also inhibited.

Freud said of obscenity that it served as a substitute for sexual aggression. Ferenczi theorized that obscene words had a capacity to evoke a type of regressive hallucinatory perception, contrary to the intellectual message of conventional words. This made possible a return to the childhood period of learning, observing and fantasizing about sex, and the intense feelings of the Oedipus complex—all repressed but simmering underneath, ready to spring into freedom at the tag line of a joke or an epithet.

Dr. Edmund Bergler felt the oral factor in humor had been neglected, that there was both oral and anal gratification when obscene words were spoken. The very mouthing of obscenity gives pleasure to the one speaking and the one listening, he said.

Wit may also be an assault via words. As a civilized man's weapon, it can be devastating. You can "kill" someone by making the world laugh at him. Remember Alice Roosevelt Longworth's description of Thomas E. Dewey when he was a Presidential candidate as "the little man on the wedding cake"?

Words may lead to violence but they seldom do if they are witty. We hold special love for those who help us laugh our way out of depression, even if they are slightly cruel in so doing.

A number of jokes unveil for the moment hostility against the parent of childhood. In his analysis of wit, Freud tells a joke in which the Emperor Augustus, noticing a remarkable resemblance between himself and a stranger in the crowd, asks the stranger, "Was your mother ever in my house?"

The stranger replies, "No, but my father was."

Jokes are akin to dreams, Freud pointed out, in that our dreams contain humor and puns.[3] (Our unconscious is extremely literal and, in analysis, the pun is taken seriously as one of the paths leading to the uncovering of unconscious conflicts.) But, as Freud said, "the dream serves preponderantly to guard against pain, while wit serves to acquire pleasure." The content of a dream is usually not comprehensible to the dreamer, for the dream is a protective device to keep us from knowing our deepest wishes; whereas the wit in humor must be comprehensible to ourselves and others if we want to laugh and want them to laugh.

Humor momentarily defeats depression as it removes the inhibition that causes a repressed feeling, by using a disguise. This disguise is often similar to the symbols that appear in our dreams, Freud pointed out. The cliché, "Many a true word is spoken in jest," shows that the underneath repression is recognized.

The disguise is tested out in the telling of a joke. If the listener laughs, showing he understands the repression, he gives permission to the one who tells the joke to laugh also. When a joke falls flat, the teller's face is the flattest thing in the room. He looks as though he had been slapped.

When we laugh, the psychic energy bound up in repression is released. It is discharged in the laughter. The chief source of pleasure in laughter is this release of energy, according to Freud. "The resultant pleasure corresponds to the economy of psychic expenditure."

Comedy differs from wit in that the latter depends on words, whereas comedy may be found in pantomime, situations or someone's behavior. In the comic situation, someone is usually made fun of, which gives the audience a sense of superiority.

We laugh when a fat man slips on a banana peel or when someone gets a pie hurled in his face. These are a child's fantasies of revenge on the giant parent. They hold the appeal of the David and Goliath story.

SENSE OF HUMOR AND MATURITY

It is difficult to laugh when you feel depressed. Then, all your energy is needed to fight the pain of living. A man awaiting execution in the death house would not be apt to chuckle at the joke Freud tells of one criminal who, on being led to his execution on a Monday, remarks, "Yes, this week is beginning well." This is what is known as "gallows humor," the ability to laugh when facing a grim scene.

Describing the difference between humor, comic pleasure and wit, Freud said that the pleasure of wit originates from an economy of expenditure in inhibition; the pleasure of the comic results from an economy of expenditure in thought; and the pleasure in humor, from an economy of expenditure in feeling.

Dr. Martin Grotjahn says that all three modes of activity of our psychic apparatus—id, ego and super-ego—"derive pleasure from economy."[4] All three strive to bring back from psychic activity

a pleasure which has really been lost in the development of this activity. For the euphoria we are thus striving to obtain is nothing but the state of a bygone time, in which we were wont to defray our psychic work with slight expenditure [before repressions set in with a vengeance]. It is the state of our childhood in which we did not know the comic, were incapable of wit, and did not need humor to make us happy.

We laugh and no longer feel depressed, because, for the moment, we can forget the grimness of reality. Our conscience will let the bars down as long as the humor does not strike directly at the heart of our deepest wishes if we believe them shameful, embarrassing or dangerous. In jokes, the weak may laugh at the strong, the fearful at the brave, and the inhibited at the free.

Theodor Reik, in analyzing the unconscious dynamics of humor, emphasizes the importance of shock and surprise. The one who listens is shocked by the emergence of a thought or wish he would never dare express seriously, but which now erupts in a disguised form that enables him to laugh.

Jokes may also be a way of turning aggression against the self. Jewish humor, analyzed by Freud and Reik, has been, according to Dr. Grotjahn (who is not Jewish) the Jews' way of saying to enemies who outnumber them so greatly they could never hope to defeat them, "You do not need to attack us. We can do that ourselves—and even better. But we can take it and we will come out all right. We know our weakness and in a way we are proud of it."

The remarkable speed with which the Jews in Israel defeated the Arab nations in the six-day war of 1967 led one Jew to observe, "At least we have shown we can be soldiers as well as masochists."

Reik disagrees with Dr. Grotjahn that the main unconscious nature of Jewish jokes is masochistic. In his book *Jewish Wit*, he says that the unconscious wish to win approval, even admiration, and, in the last analysis, the deep desire to gain "or better, to regain love," is part of the masochistic character of the Jewish wit.[5] Quite apart from the fact that there are numerous jokes in which a self-degrading and self-mocking characteristic does not appear, others show overconfidence and even impudence, Reik says.

He believes that a feeling of paranoia is just as important as masochism in understanding Jewish wit. "There is an oscillation between masochistic self-humiliation and paranoid superiority." (Once again, Melanie Klein's theory of the paranoid and depressive positions intertwined would seem to apply.)

There are Irish jokes and Negro jokes and today even

Martian jokes, which reflect a mockery of what is feared. The men from Mars are always portrayed as tiny, gnomelike creatures without much power. Jokes about the Irish usually center on religion or drinking or birth control. Jokes about the Negro focus on sex, showing the white man's fear that the Negro has greater sexual prowess. Many jokes mirror scorn—a well-known defense against envy and fear.

Sometimes what one person thinks funny another will not. The victim of teasing or of a practical joke may boil in rage as others laugh. He may become depressed as he holds back his anger. He may want to kill the jokester but dares not express his anger because he does not want to be thought a poor sport, one of the greatest unofficial crimes in America.

It is difficult to laugh at the self. The less dramatically we take life, the more we can see the self as occasionally a laughing matter. But we seldom appreciate someone else laughing at us. Children, particularly, feel humiliated and angry when adults laugh at them.

A little girl of six was riding in an open motorboat on a beautiful, sunny day but then a brisk wind stirred up waves so the boat kept bouncing up and down. Her father turned to a slightly seasick visitor and said reassuringly, "It's really a very calm day."

The little girl remarked, "It may be a calm day, but it sure is a rough ocean."

Everyone on the boat burst into laughter except the little girl, who burst into tears. She thought they were laughing at her, not her joke.

Where does laughter start? Child psychologists have studied the baby and observed that a smile which shows acceptance and pleasure may appear as early as the eighth day of life. During the first six months, the infant is likely to smile indiscriminately at everyone. Then he starts to discriminate between his mother and the stranger. He may welcome both, or only one, with a smile.

If a baby loses his ability to smile, he is depressed. For the inability to smile shows emotional starvation and lack of human contact, according to Dr. Spitz. It may lead in extreme cases to mental or physical death.

A sense of humor signifies emotional maturity, as well as affording relief from depression. It indicates we have accepted as best we can the repressions in ourselves, our faults and our idiosyncrasies. As we laugh, we enjoy a healthy, swift return to earlier fantasies. We also enjoy the release of energy not at the moment needed for repression.

But laughter and tears can be very close. As the Bible says, "Even in laughter the heart is sorrowful."

THE CLOWN MAY BE SAD

In order to be able to laugh, either at the humor of others or at our own sometimes ridiculous self, we have to possess a fair amount of what analysts call "ego strength," or self-esteem. Those whose self-respect is low find it hard, if not impossible, to lift themselves out of depression into the heights of humor.

Just as with the creative spirit, the person who is a comic spirit may suffer depression. While facing an audience he may appear to have beaten the blues. But when he retires to his dressing room or den, he becomes proof of the "laugh, clown, laugh" adage. He is lonely and defeated when the mask of laughter is removed.

The late Bert Lahr, among the greatest of comedians, would blurt out, "Some fun, hey kid?" as he pranced wildly about the stage. Then offstage, a few moments later, he turned into a melancholy, shy, superstitious, worried and hypochondriacal man, according to his obituary in *The New York Times*. The obituary stated: "For him, his years in the theater were a dogged, lifelong struggle against myopic critics, fickle audiences and the horror of obscurity."

"I am a sad man," Lahr once said. "A plumber doesn't go out with his tools. Does a comedian have to be funny on the street?"

He worried endlessly about his shows. Even success troubled him. He told a friend, after a smash hit, who asked him why he was so anxious, "Where am I going to find a book and score to follow this up? This show is so good that I'm ruined forever."

The clown, and to a lesser degree all optimists in contrast to pessimists, clings to the illusion that he can still live as a baby. He acts as if he has the "good mother" to take care of him, ignoring the harsh demands of reality.

"Optimists live as if life offers them a drink or a breast to nurse from," says Dr. Grotjahn. "They often look like satisfied babies. They are trusting children who expect some powerful mother to step forth in the future to feed them. 'Everything will be all right,' is their slogan. They are the noble characters who never learn from bad experience. They will smile when the realist frowns."

Psychoanalysts find that the overoptimistic souls, while on the couch, reveal the underlying depression. They are angry, frightened, unsure of themselves.

Pessimists are difficult to live with, but then so are optimists, for they also push reality aside. Pessimists see life as too cruel, optimists as too giving.

The true humorist looks at himself, accepts himself as he is and does not take too seriously society's shibboleths. Today's humorist even makes fun of psychoanalysis. A recent cartoon in *Playboy* shows a psychoanalyst reaching out from his chair behind the couch and striking with his fist the head of the patient lying on the couch, as he says, "Maybe *that* will knock some sense into you."

This holds "surprise and shock," in Reik's words, because it is what an analyst would *never* do. It goes against every principle of psychoanalysis. A patient would be stunned out of his remaining wits if an analyst ever struck him.

The joke also shows projected aggression, mirroring the wish of the patient to hit the analyst at times as the latter perhaps is revealing too much of the painful truth. Also, it is funny because those in analysis know how very difficult it is to acquire insight about the self and occasionally would welcome being able to get it with a simple blow on the head.

Playboy strikes out at psychoanalysis as a target in another cartoon, which shows a woman sitting on the analytic couch, her shoes and jacket off, buttoning up her blouse. Behind her a bearded analyst is stuffing his shirt into his trousers as his tie, notebook and pencil lie on the chair. The caption reads: "Should I tell you about this in my next session, Doctor?"

This cartoon reflects every patient's unconscious wish to have sexual intimacy with the analyst (in the unconscious, he is the mother and/or father of infancy). It also knocks the pedantic parent off his pedestal of virtue.

Psychoanalysts do not mind being laughed at. They are glad when people laugh, knowing this is preferable to feeling depressed.

III

×××××××××××××××××××

*Dealing with
Depression*

8

◇◇◇◇◇◇◇◇◇◇◇◇◇◇◇◇◇◇◇◇◇◇◇◇◇◇◇◇◇◇◇◇◇◇◇◇

Depression at Certain Stages

As psychoanalysts, starting with Freud, have explored the causes of depression, the distinction has come into being between sadness and depression. In sadness, or occasional moodiness, there is no guilt, therefore no need to punish the self and no devaluation of the self. There is no guilt because sadness and moods are related to reality. But depression, which stems from fantasy, holds an inner guilt because of the secret wish to kill.

Because of this secret wish *and* the belief in the magic power of the wish (that the wish is the same as the deed), we may become depressed as a way of punishing the self for daring to harbor such an evil wish.

All of us face getting over a belief in magic, which is part of childhood. The more emotionally painful the childhood, the more imperfect and hateful the parents seem, and the greater will be the need for magic (the weaker we feel, the greater our need for magical power).

Every child at one time or another will hate his parents, as well as love them. And when he hates, he magically thinks murder, for in our unconscious, hate carries with it an "off with his head" order. We have to learn not to feel guilty about the early childhood wish to murder our parents. (This is the fascination of a Lizzie Borden case, although it must be remembered that it was her stepmother she killed, which may have made it easier for her.)

Each time you hate, unconsciously you wish to murder

151

and may feel guilty. Except that what you feel guilty
about is not the present wish alone, but also the wished-
for murders of the past.

You have to realize it is perfectly natural to feel like
murdering someone who has hurt you. As long as you do
not commit the murder, you need not feel guilty. A wish
never killed anyone, although some primitive peoples
who stick pins into small images of the one they wish
dead believe they have the power to kill via the wish.

First there is rage repressed, then the turning of the
rage on the self. This is depression in a nutshell, or as
near a nutshell as we can get, for there is really no such
thing as "nutshell" when we speak of the psyche. It is too
full of wishes, memories, fears, angers, hopes and
dreams.

One reason we may feel depressed in the morning is
the fear of our own repressed rage and aggression. We
need a certain amount of aggression to get through the day
but then there is aggression over and above what is required for work, caused by our secret rage at others. This
fury sometimes appears indirectly in our dreams. This is
another reason some find it difficult to get moving in the
morning. Their dreams leave them paralyzed as they
wake near to their unconscious, which dimly conveys to
them the awful truth of their murderous and sexual desires.

Why do some become very depressed, others not?
Psychoanalysts believe that those who hate excessively as
children, which means those who receive little love from
their parents (whose emotionally disturbed parents unduly
thwart and defy them and set unfortunate examples), will
be full of murderous wishes. They will then feel guilty,
turn the murder inward and punish themselves by im-
mobilizing and paralyzing emotions and deeds.

Everyone as a child, at one time or another, is apt to
hate and wish to kill a parent, then feel guilty and
depressed. All the ages of man, from then on, can
hold depression. Depression may even become a way of
life for some (the whole of life can be a mosaic of misery
if one permits it to be). For others, mild depression may

occur at moments of crises, when major decisions have to be made, or traumatic events occur, or there are severe physical changes in the body.

ANXIETY AT ADOLESCENCE

One of these times is adolescence. It is then that a slight snub from a classmate may take on the tragic overtones of a spear to the heart. Or a date that is not kept can plummet a boy or girl into thoughts of suicide.

Adolescence is accepted as a time of torment and rebellion. Parents and teachers, perhaps too glibly, dismiss the extreme moods with a shrug of the shoulders and the feeling, "It's natural at this age."

It may be frequent but that does not make it natural, if it is an extreme or lasting depression. For natural growth does not encompass long periods of intense despair or riotous rebellion, but rather an exhilarating excitement about growing up, in spite of conflicts about leaving childhood.

The adolescent finds ways to fight his depression. He can study very hard and try to blot out his anxiety. He can exert himself in sports. Or he can become destructive and, aping his elders, take to drink or drugs.

Why drugs? The users of LSD tell us why. "Life comes alive," says a college student. "I can *feel*—the intensity of a color or a bar of music." Comments another, "You just float along, man, enjoying the simple things." They settle for the gratifying of fantasy rather than true accomplishment.

Why is adolescence a time when depression may strike? Most adolescents when they reach sixteen or seventeen are faced with leaving the comfort and security given by a mother, father, sister and brother (no matter how horrendous a family life may be, it is always familiar and familial, and therefore dear). This separation also revives earlier depressions that followed on minor separations. Memories of these depressions are usually buried during the years between seven and thirteen as the boy or girl puts energy and attention into his schoolwork, sports, social activities and relations with other children.

But the adolescent now must venture out on his own into what is called not so jestingly the "cold, cruel world." He either goes to college, business school or work. A few, but increasingly fewer, girls will sit at home marking time until they marry.

Going to college for most boys and girls means giving up their family. Most meet this challenge successfully but it can fill a high school senior with anxiety as to whether he will succeed.

Also, adolescence is a time when sexual urges, relatively quiet since six or seven, suddenly surge up with what may be overwhelming intensity. Therefore, in addition to the emotional problems he faces, the adolescent has biological problems, as Dr. Rhoda Lorand, a psychoanalyst who specializes in the treatment of children and adolescents, points out.[1]

This body, with which he has long been very familiar, rather suddenly becomes an adult body with a strikingly different appearance. He must learn to know himself and to feel at home with his radically changed outer envelope which forms a most important part of his ideas about himself. And he must learn to feel in control, and not at the mercy, of the strong sexual feelings which flood his body, create erotic fantasies in his mind and impel him to seek ever-increasing contact with the opposite sex.

She divides most teenage problems into three categories:

1. Anxiety in relation to the "new" body: difficulties in achieving a firm sense of identity as male or female.

2. Anxiety about the greatly increased sexual feelings: the degree and manner of their expression.

3. Conflicts about remaining safely dependent upon the parents as in the past, versus striking out for independence in all areas: transfer of affection outside the

family, establishment of an individual moral code and finding one's life work.

She believes the most important task the adolescent must accomplish is to find someone outside his family to love. She says that one of the reasons moodiness, depression and feelings of loneliness and despair are so common in the adolescent "is that the young person often has moments of feeling desperately alone and longs for new love ties which have not yet been established."

But before he can find someone to love, she explains, he must first break childhood ties of love to his parents, brothers and sisters. This does not mean that he stops loving them, only that he eventually loves them in a different way. No longer is he the little child idolizing the great parent whose every word he accepts as truth. During adolescence "he must decide for himself whether he fully agrees with their principles, ethics, morals, ideals, goals and standards." By the time he reaches young adulthood, according to Dr. Lorand, the antagonism and rebellion which inevitably accompany the shift from childhood to maturity should have disappeared. The former rebel should feel he is a loving friend and equal of his parents.

She points out that some parents do not understand fully the need for a child's break with the family. Particularly in situations where they have leaned too heavily on their children's love, perhaps because of inadequacies within the marriage, parents may feel a sense of deprivation and abandonment as they see the youngster transfer his love and allegiance elsewhere. "And this process is to some degree a painful experience for every adolescent," Dr. Lorand comments, "no matter how callous he may appear."

The adolescent physically and mentally is an adult, but emotionally is part child, part adult. This is shown in his attitude toward sex. On the one hand, he is beset with the idea of "romantic" love (a concept of love which many so-called adults never progress beyond) as he idealizes members of the opposite sex beyond all possible reality. On the other hand, he is faced with the need to come to terms with his sensual feelings, which may at times be so intense that he becomes preoccupied with sex to the exclusion of all else.

The adolescent has to learn the value of tenderness if he wishes to be happy with someone he loves. Unless he does, as Freud warned, he will not be able to give love. Sensual feelings alone will not ensure permanent love.

If adolescents have grown up in homes where they have observed and absorbed tender feelings exchanged between parents, they will be likely to offer tenderness to others.

Depression in adolescence, as at any other age, can be either openly displayed, lying in wait to break out or masked, according to Dr. Maurice R. Green.[2] He says:

It can be neurotic, borderline or psychotic; associated with any other physical or mental illness or existing in almost pure culture as an entity in itself . . . It may appear to be a "realistic" response to the actually unfortunate circumstances of one's race, social class, heredity, or immediate environment. The depression may be expressed in the form of shallow or very profound criticism of one's parents, society, or even humanity itself. It may be expressed through a variety of aggressive, defiant and disobedient behaviors, or it may be expressed through a variety of physical symptoms, psychological reactions, and neurotic or regressive symptoms.

The combination of "vulnerability" and "promise" so characteristic of adolescent years makes the adolescent especially attractive to adults for exploitation and identification or simply love and admiration, Dr. Green says. He adds, "The fact that teen-age taste sets the fashion in dance, music, clothes, cars, and so many other facets of our popular mass market, raises questions about our so-called adult society."

The adolescent must be helped to affirm the ties and continuities he chooses from the past of his juvenile and childhood life with his family, at the same time he is supported in cutting off those aspects from which he chooses to free himself, Dr. Green points out. He must be helped to face the future responsibilities and be prevented from evading "the complexities of his confusion, rebellion, love and pride which often cripple him in his everyday decisions."

The psychic pressures of adolescence may be so drastic for the troubled that they cannot cope with them. In the past decade the suicide rate for college students has more than doubled.

On the American campus, suicide has become the Number 2 killer, just below accidents. The rate for adolescent suicide in the nation (ages fifteen to nineteen) jumped from 2.4 per 100,000 in 1954 to 4 per 100,000 in 1964, the last year for which statistics are complete. In 1964, 1736 adolescents killed themselves and it was estimated that, since there are supposed to be ten attempts for every finished act, there were 17,360 who tried suicide (of children fourteen years and younger, 180 killed themselves; officials of the National Education Association believe there are at least twice as many child suicides each year as are reported on the police blotters).

Suicides run higher among college students by a full 50 per cent than for Americans in general. Suicide is nearly half again as frequent among college students as among those of the same age who are not in college.

It is not unusual to see headlines in a newspaper telling of an adolescent who has killed himself. Sometimes he will not want to live when he is caught doing something wrong, as in the case of the eighteen-year-old son of a well-known New York family when arrested on a charge of possession of narcotics. He hung himself at the jail to which he was taken with a necktie he had knotted around the bars of his cell.

Leif J. Braaten, Ph.D., and Dr. C. Douglas Darling studied 630 students from the general campus population at Cornell University during the academic year of 1960–61.[3] These students sought help from the mental health division at the university because of emotional problems.

Every tenth student, to a greater or lesser degree, was concerned about suicide. Sixty-six per cent said they had "occasional thoughts" of suicide; 68 per cent had "occa-

sional thoughts or impulses on a rather intellectual level";
27 per cent had "rather frequent and intensive inclina-
tions" toward suicide, although they made no attempt
other than minor acts of self-mutilation; and 5 per cent
made attempts to destroy themselves completely. The authors of the article point out that some who made the
attempts did not admit ever thinking about it.

In the order of frequency, the attempts took the form
of: poisonous drugs, "jumping the gorge" (this meant
jumping off one of the two rather deep gorges that run
through the Cornell campus area), gas poisoning in apart-
ment or car, shooting, cutting with razor blades, hanging
and car accident.

Those who tried to kill themselves made on the average
two attempts each. "Therefore, the risk of a repeated
suicide attempt should not be underestimated," the authors warned.

The common characteristics of those who tried suicide
were: anger, hostility and excessive competitiveness; excessive dependency; moderate to severe depression; fears
about masculinity or femininity; crises in love attachments; severe study difficulties; and self-hate.

There do exist in college the pressures of getting high
grades, being popular, joining the right fraternity or
sorority. There is also the pressure of being on one's own,
having to make all the decisions formerly made by a
mother and father. This will be hard for the boy or girl
who has been overprotected or overdominated at home,
never allowed to achieve much independence while growing up.

If there has been too deep a dependency, the young
person who reluctantly takes a few of his treasures and
clothes in a couple of suitcases and sets off for college will
feel as though he is going to his own execution. It is such
a boy or girl who, if he has an unhappy love affair in college, or fails an examination, or is unable to make friends,
is most likely to wish himself dead.

One boy of eighteen, who hanged himself in his fraternity house, left behind a note to his parents which in-
formed them: "Lila told me she didn't love me any more

and I don't want to live without her, so I am killing myself. I know you will understand."

The distraught mother, who did *not* understand, sought a psychiatrist's help to try to overcome her grief. She talked at length about her son.

"We had to *fight* to get him to go to college," she sobbed. "He didn't *want* to leave us but we made him. He fell desperately in love with this pretty girl, Lila, who was in his class. We thought everything was going fine. Then this happened. I don't understand it at all, although he wrote that I would."

The psychiatrist pointed out, "You said, 'We had to fight to get him to go to college. He didn't *want* to leave us.' "

"But he *had* to," she protested. "His father would have died if his son weren't a college graduate."

"But the boy died instead," the psychiatrist said quietly. "He wasn't ready to leave you. He told you so."

"What should we have done?" wailed the mother. "What did we do wrong?"

"You might have helped your son to get psychiatric treatment before going to college, or even while he was there, since you knew how upset he felt about leaving you," said the psychiatrist.

Comparatively few adolescents feel this extreme a depression. But in moderate degree they may face some of the same conflicts. We do not know how deeply involved this boy was with the girl but the young person who is supersensitive cannot bear feeling someone no longer loves him.

Actually this boy, in killing himself, according to psychoanalytic theory, was in part killing the mother of his infancy for her rejection of him (either real or fancied or both). When he was sent away to college, he again felt rejected. The girl's rejection toppled completely this unhappy boy's mountain of misery.

The turbulent time of adolescence may be made even more difficult if the family pattern is in any way disturbed—if the mother and father get a divorce or if a sister or brother marries or if anyone in the family dies. A death, especially, may send an emotionally disturbed adolescent into a tailspin.

One man of thirty-two, who went into analysis because he had never been able to get married and felt like a freak, was talking about an older brother who had been killed in an automobile crash when he was twenty and the patient fourteen. The brother had just announced his engagement and planned to be married within six months.

As the patient recalled the fatal crash, tears came into his eyes. He said, "How tragic, that my brother should die on the eve of his marriage."

Then he said, in sudden insight, "I think I have felt ever since the crash that if I wanted to get married, I would die too."

This had been one of his fantasies, that marriage equaled death. Underlying this fantasy whirled a number of hidden emotions, including childhood hatred of his older, more handsome brother. So that when his brother died, he had the additional fantasy that he had killed him and therefore did not deserve to get married and find the happiness his victim had been denied. He had been suffering over the years because of his guilt, an unreal one.

Two major decisions face the young man or woman reaching twenty-one: what kind of work to undertake for life, and who to marry for life. It is important to choose work that is satisfying. As Dr. Leo Rangell, past president of the American Psychoanalytic Association, put it: "The person who gets up and hates the way he's going to spend the day, won't spend his evening very happily."[4] The importance of choosing the right mate is obvious, as far as future happiness is concerned.

There are real reasons today, in addition to the unreal wishes of the world of fantasy, why adolescents might feel depressed. Young men face military service and young women face losing a boyfriend or husband to the armed forces. This naturally does not provide a happy aura for adolescence. It is one cause of the increasing number of marriages between young people who feel they must snatch some moments of happiness before they are torn apart.

Yet the world has never been a very secure place in which to live. The adolescent growing up in the days of the caveman might not survive the next few hours if his father could not find food as he roamed the hills or forests in search of wild animals. The adolescent growing up in this country in its pioneer days, living under the terror of anticipated Indian raids and massacres, could not have felt very safe.

The adolescent can try to understand some of the conflicts that may be upsetting him so he may solve them rationally. He can try to use his great supply of energy in wise fashion, not paralyzing it in drugs or dissipating it in other wasteful activity. If he feels he needs psychological help, he would do well to seek it, for the earlier in life he receives treatment, the shorter it is likely to be and the easier it is to use.

As Dr. Green says, "Effective help at this time may accomplish in a shorter period what is so difficult and sometimes impossible to do in later adult life—prevent the recurrence of paralyzing despair and constricting self-depreciatory rumination."

The adolescent can accept that the days of childhood are past, that adulthood can be exciting even if life is not all whipped cream. He can recognize that he will have to study hard and work hard at a job. He will have to give much thought to the kind of career he wants and equal thought to the kind of woman (or man) with whom the rest of his life will be spent, raising a family.

Parents can help by knowing what their teen-ager is going through as he shifts from childhood into adulthood. Dr. Rhoda Lorand's book *Love, Sex and the Teenager* will give valuable insights as will *Adolescents: Psychoanalytic Approach to Problems and Therapy,* edited by Dr. Sandor Lorand and Dr. Henry Schneer.

Parents can also help by treating their adolescent children with dignity and courtesy, realizing they are well on their way to maturity. Above all, parents can be aware that adolescence is a time of oversensitivity and not take personally some of the expressed sentiments of their children which might seem, at the moment, cruel and uncaring.

They should remember, as Anna Freud wrote, speaking of adolescent behavior, that

Adolescence is by its nature an interruption of peaceful growth . . . it is normal for an adolescent to behave for a considerable length of time in an inconsistent and unpredictable manner; to fight his impulses and to accept them; to love his parents and to hate them; to revolt against them and to be dependent on them; to be deeply ashamed to acknowledge his mother before others and, unexpectedly, to desire heart to heart talks with her . . . to be more idealistic, artistic, generous and unselfish than he will ever be again, but also the opposite: self-centered, egoistic, calculating . . .[5]

If an adolescent becomes too depressed, his parents would be wise to suggest he get help. A growing number of psychiatrists and psychoanalysts today specialize in adolescent treatment. The first national organization of its kind, The American Society for Adolescent Psychiatry, was organized recently by five hundred psychiatrists from thirty states.

In the face of need, colleges are adding mental health services, although only 76 of the nation's 2252 colleges and universities have campus clinics. Only about 100 others have a psychiatrist available part time.

More students are seeking psychiatric help than ever before. A recent study by Dr. Clifford Bruce Reifler, Dr. J. Thomas Fox and Dr. Myron B. Liptzin at the University of North Carolina showed that the number of students seen regularly for emotional disorder at the university had increased 10 per cent per year during the past ten years. This is a rate faster than the growth of the university. The study also found that women students use the university's mental health clinic more frequently than men.

A study of students who dropped out of Harvard for emotional reasons was reported by Dr. Armand Nicholi.[6]

He said that dropouts were suffering from depression and described the latter as "related to an awareness of the disparity between one's ideal self as a uniquely gifted intellectual achiever and the real self as one of thousands of outstanding students struggling in a vigorously competitive environment." This awareness, he said, resulted in feelings of worthlessness and reduced self-esteem.

The Harvard study also revealed that emotional disorders were four times more prevalent among all dropouts than among the general undergraduate population.

The treatment of choice for the depressed adolescent is that of psychoanalysis, according to Dr. Sandor Lorand, who has treated a number of adolescents. But successful treatment is possible only if the adolescent is willing to accept it.

Dr. Lorand says that the painful psychic achievement of the adolescent, which is "his detachment from parental authority," is so painful precisely because "he experiences it not as a liberation but as an abandonment by those objects on whom he relies for guidance and support. Hence the reluctance sets in, accompanied by feelings of aloneness, emptiness, and helplessness, and a resentment towards the idea of abandoning the past."[7]

The adolescent's inability to function, if he is a dropout or fails to achieve high marks, serves as a "realistic if not desirable means of maintaining his ties to the family." The adolescent, according to Dr. Lorand,

is preoccupied with ideas of revenge and violent hatred. He tries to discharge the aggression and desire for revenge upon himself and, at the same time, hurt the tormenting object. He revenges himself on the incorporated object, destroys the object, and punishes himself for this revenge, expiating his guilt feelings by self-destruction and also eliminating the hated object.

The need for compliance to the demands of his own conscience and to reality, on the one hand, and his rebellion against those pressures and demands, on the other, produce a steady conflict with feelings of guilt which sustain the depression, Dr. Lorand explains.

It is heartening that more and more young people are seeking therapy as they realize they cannot fight the battle alone. They do not want to be emotionally crippled for the rest of their lives.

MIDDLE-AGE MOODS

Another time in life when depression may occur is middle age. The late forties and fifties are dreaded by some, particularly those who may have had depressions before. For the depressed person hates to let go of his youth, since part of his problem is that he is still living too much in it in fantasy.

At this stage of life, the grass is likely to look greener in other places than home. A husband may start to wander, believing he might as well explore sexually while he still has the energy. A wife may ask, as her children leave for college or to work and to get married, "Is this all there is going to be to my life?"

Middle age also means menopause for women, who sometimes sink into depression because they are unable to bear more babies. They may feel unglamorous, sexless.

Men may fear they are losing their potency. It is at this time that marriages may shatter as the man seeks a younger woman as wife because he thinks she will help him be more virile.

But, as psychoanalysts point out, if one's life before has been filled with friendship, love and understanding of others, middle age will hold no special terror. It will also be a time of growth. With children out of the house, parents who are happy with each other should be able to enjoy their new leisure.

Middle age, sometimes called "the critical age," presents a challenge to both men and women, according to Dr. Alberta B. Szalita.[8] The menopause, lasting for weeks in some cases and up to several years in others, causes more of an upheaval for the woman. But once through with this time of her life, she can settle down to a more or less peaceful life more easily than the man, Dr. Szalita maintains.

Middle age has also been called "the involutional age." Dr. Szalita says:

For neither sex does involution take place without despair and regret. Nor is their involution without struggle. But struggle, regret and despair are active emotions of the process of mourning and grief; active psychodynamic forces lead, in the final analysis, to a solution, to a new distribution of energy and interests, and to acceptable and often an enjoyable senescence.

When hopelessness and helplessness prevail, the outcome is "fearful surrender." Whether someone accepts the conflicts of middle age with ease or with difficulty depends, she says, on the development of the person, the experiences of his life and his lifelong habits of dealing with stress.

The menopause may occur between the ages of forty-five and fifty-three. The average age, according to authorities, is forty-seven. Sexual desire in women may remain unaffected during this period. Investigators have observed that sexual desire persists in a heightened degree for many years after menopause, once the woman has successfully overcome feelings of depression that may be part of the menopause.

Dr. Szalita holds that menopause is invariably perceived as trauma by women. "The fearful anticipation in puberty always contains a certain measure of hope, whereas the anxious anticipation in menopause is hopeless," she says.

While men may also become depressed at the thought of approaching old age, the man is compensated because he can achieve even greater success at this stage of his life, either in business or other professional activities, she says. Some men even discover themselves at this time, such as Sherwood Anderson and Paul Gauguin, who, at the approach of middle age, suddenly decided they did not like their life the way it was, changed it, and became famous.

A "different kind of courage" is needed at this stage of life, according to Dr. Szalita. It is the courage "to admit one's frailties and to make the wisest use of one's equipment."

Men and women "are compelled" to confront their lives slipping away. They may go through anguish and confusion, as they answer such questions as: "What have I done with my life? What am I going to do from now on? What did I expect from life? What is the meaning of life?" Dr. Szalita declares.

Some will "surrender to fear," in her words. But others, "blessed with a disposition and a way of life that make them proud of living," will "count the passing years among their foremost riches."

THE ACHES OF OLD AGE

Then there is the depression of old age which may sweep over a person, one from which he may never recover. Old age may be grim if the years preceding it have not held much pleasure. The supposedly golden years, our last on earth, may turn out for some to be years of blackness.

But old age does not have to be a time of depression. It was Plato who said, "He who is of a calm and happy nature will hardly feel the pressure of age, but to him who is of an opposite disposition youth and age are equally a burden." He wrote this in 329 B.C. and it still holds today.

And as Voltaire said, "He who has not the spirit of his age, of his age has all the misery."

There is a "spirit" to old age for those who have lived wisely in their choice of loved ones and in their choice of work. We see such people in the world and it does not matter whether they are rich or poor. They have reached the seventies, eighties and even nineties with the same self-confidence and grace with which they have gone through the earlier years.

Someone once said, "Old age is the same—only more so." The person who has always been depressed, upon realizing he nears the end of a life that has held little happiness, is apt to become slightly more depressed. But there is many an aging person who gets up each morning as cheerfully as he ever did, who continues a life that is challenging and productive, who lives with a mate he loves. No generalities can be made about "the aged," just as no generalities can be made about any other group, for each individual must be considered in terms of his own life.

There are real reasons, however, that may cause depression in old age. The older we grow, the more we are apt to see the people we love die, and the natural processes of mourning take over automatically.

"The older one gets, the more one experiences the loss of significant persons. The aging person has, of necessity, to undergo more and more grief reactions." These are the words of Dr. Martin A. Berezin, who, with Dr. Stanley H. Cath, has edited several books for the aged and their children who are concerned about them, including *Geriatric Psychiatry: Grief, Loss, and Emotional Disorders in the Aging Process.* (Another helpful book is *You and Your Aging Parents,* by Edith M. Stern with Mabel Ross, M.D.)

Dr. Berezin points out that the aged suffer losses not encountered earlier in life. These fall into three groups: job, status and money; bodily functions and abilities, such as loss of sight, or hearing, sexual drive, locomotion; and loss of independence and self-respect.

These losses "are invariably encountered in varying degrees by all aged people," says Dr. Berezin.

Depressive illness tends to increase with age, according to Dr. Sidney Levin, a psychoanalyst who has worked with the aged, in a special interview. Suicide becomes a progressively more frequent occurrence with advancing years, but it is less well recognized that the milder forms of depression are also more common in the aged, he points out. They also tend to take a form somewhat different from that usually found in younger persons, for they are characterized primarily by a state of apathy. Older depressed persons "are apt to sit around with a somewhat vacant stare on their faces, appearing preoccupied."

Thus, age may be a period of crisis when new problems must be met, occurring at a time when the person may feel his spirit sagging and when both his family and society may seem exceptionally cold and cruel. A number of the aged give up trying and sink into the depression that leads to death. The suicide rate for the aged is very high.

Dr. Martin Grotjahn, who has studied the psychological processes of aging and carried on psychoanalytic treatment of the aged, says there are three different ways a person can react to the problem of aging.[9]

The first is the normal solution, which aims at the acceptance "of a life as it has been lived" and the integration of old age with that life.

The second reaction is an increased rigidity and conservatism of the ego as it tries to hold the line of defenses according to the pattern of previous more or less neurotic adjustment.

The third reaction is a neurotic and often a psychotic regression.

Growing old, particularly in this country, where so much emphasis is placed on keeping young and beautiful, may be felt as a wound to self-esteem and further denigration of the image of the self as the face grows wrinkled, the hair turns gray and the tendency to live for eating alone puts on added pounds.

Psychologically, as Dr. Grotjahn points out, age is often felt as repeating the threat of castration. He maintains that the neuroses of old age may be a defense against castration anxiety, in part.

"Our unconscious has no knowledge, no representation of our own death," he says.

Because there is no knowledge in the unconscious of our own death, "this explains the lack of time, space and logic within the primary process of the unconscious," he continues.

Our unconscious knows all about the death, mutilation and murder of others. Our unconscious also knows the dangers of mutilation and castration which we anticipate with fear and anxiety. In the psychotherapy of elderly people, these castration anxieties have to be analyzed before death anxiety can be dealt with.

Overwhelming fear of death in the elderly hides castration anxiety and may lead to the desire to die. It is extremely important in the practice of psychotherapy with the elderly to realize that a good part of death anxiety is a symbolic representation of castration anxiety activated by the narcissistic trauma of aging.

But there are some aspects in the psychology of aging that seem to make psychotherapy easier, he says. For one, resistance against unpleasant insights about the self is frequently less in old age. The demands of reality, which in earlier years may have been flung aside, are finally accepted.

"It seems as if more or less suddenly resistance is weakened and insight occurs just because it is 'high time,' " Dr. Grotjahn puts it.

The attitude of contemplation and retrospection in old age may, with the help of the therapist, be turned into an attitude of introspection, which then sometimes constitutes the start and basis of understanding and therapy.

The task of integrating one's life as it has been lived and the final acceptance of one's own death are problems of existence. To deal with them is the great task of old age. They are essentially different from the tasks of infancy, childhood, adolescence, and maturity . . . Final self-acceptance is not naively given—as in infancy—but now must become a conscious achievement.

Electroshock treatment may be successful in some cases because "shock treatment may provide a deepgoing experience of death with a happy ending," he theorizes. It may, for some, be a realistic experience that they can live "beyond and after castration."

In two cases which he treated by daily analytic interviews, who also received electroshock treatment, it seemed to him, he said, "as if the spectacular recovery symbolized an acceptance of the unacceptable but unavoidable end."

The son or daughter of an aging parent often has many new conflicts to face, some realistic, some unrealistic. If there is physical illness, he must arrange for the care of his parent, which may be costly and last a long time. Sometimes there is no alternative but a nursing home. This he must choose wisely, for although there are many excellent nursing homes in the country, some are inadequate both in the food and facilities they supply and in their understanding of the emotional needs of the aged.

The psychological implications of an aging parent unable to take care of himself are serious ones for his children. They are now the parent figure and he has become the child. The "magic" is gone, the omnipotence of the parent finally destroyed, and the child, if he has not done so, must grow up enough emotionally so he *can* take care of the parent, as the parent once did him.

The child now has to "baby" and "humor" the parent, accept his physical and psychological infirmities and do all he can to make his parent comfortable. Those who have been overly dependent on a parent have to try not to sink into a depression similar to the parent's out of their identification with the parent.

Dr. Alvin Goldfarb, one of the country's leading psychiatrists in the treatment of the aged, makes the point that openly "senile" behavior may serve as the facade for depression and withdrawal. There may be mental impairment but frequently it is exaggerated by emotional stress.[10]

Understanding an aging parent's conflicts does not mean that the child must take the parent under his roof. Dr. Goldfarb warns against children feeling they must live with an aging parent at all cost.

It is not advisable for parent and child to live together, Dr. Goldfarb and other psychiatrists point out. The child cannot solve the parent's problems and the parent is likely to make it even more difficult in the home of the child, causing dissension among husbands and wives and their children.

A ten-year-old girl recently wrote a letter to a columnist who gives answers to family problems. The little girl stated:

My grandmother lives with us and she is always bawling us out no matter what we do. She thinks of bad things that could happen to us like she does not want us to go anywhere by car because there was an accident here that happened about a year before and it killed everyone in it. We can't walk to school alone because some bad guy might pick us up. She fights all the time with my mother about what is good for us. What in Heaven's name should we do?

If we have an aging parent, we have to make sure that the guilt we feel, which stems from childhood wishes to kill, does not lead us into situations that will bring both the parent and ourselves further unhappiness.

In many instances, aging parents need only a little money to be able to live by themselves, and sons and daughters are able to furnish this. In other cases, where custodial care is needed, the son or daughter must search for the best possible nursing home. For those who cannot afford such care, low-cost facilities are available, usually sponsored by religious or governmental groups. The government will take care of the aged who have no resources except Social Security and the money they receive under Old Age Assistance.

Today there is growing emphasis on what is called rehabilitation for the aged, not in the deepest psychological sense, but in trying to fill their hours with recreation and whatever work they are capable of doing. Housing developments are springing up, dedicated to making life more pleasurable for the aged who wish to live with each other.

There is no reason, other than unrealistic ones, based on past guilts, why a child must suffer because he has an aging parent. As a matter of fact, the parent will feel better if he is receiving the care he needs, both physical and psychological, at the hands of professional workers who know what they do.

Those who have depressed parents are apt, out of their own unresolved conflicts, to hurt them further, rather than help, if they try to cope with their parents' emotional problems as well as their own. They should visit parents, if the latter live in their own home with a companion or elsewhere, as often as they can, not out of guilt but because they know the visits bring pleasure to the parent, no matter how depressed he may be.

9

×>×<×>×<×>×<×>×<×>×<×>×<×>×<×>×<×>×<×>×<×>×<×>×<×>×<×

Easing Depression:
Action and Self-knowledge

Can we do anything by ourselves to ease depression if
we accept that depression is caused by events and fantasies of infancy, and accept, too, that these events and
fantasies may be largely unconscious by now?

Is it not true that if we could reach the unconscious
alone we would, indeed, do so, and then we would all be
as happy as those proverbial kings? But instead, are not
cabbages still cabbages, and the unconscious still the
unconscious, available only with the help of a psychoanalyst?

Thus asks Dr. Karl Menninger.[1] Referring to those
who become unduly angry to an extent which we recognize as mentally unhealthy, and to others who get "painfully depressed," he says:

Now, can such a person by giving thought to the matter,
and by constantly wanting to change it and trying to do so,
accomplish anything? In other words, can a man really learn
to control his temper, and can a man with the "blues" lift
himself by his own boot-straps? Can such individuals by
making a deliberate effort to do so prevent these tendencies
from going to the extreme of such a mental collapse as
melancholia?

He answers: "I think they can. I think everyone knows
they can. But everyone also knows that they often don't.

All of us know golfers who continue to lose tournaments because they get so angry or depressed over a bad shot or a bad break in the luck that they lose their poise."

Dr. Menninger warns that the danger of giving credence to the theory that, in some measure, our own mind can control itself is "that it lends ammunition to the quacks and is carried to extremes."

It has given rise to a flock of cheer-'em-up books, most of which are not worth the paper they are written on. It is the thesis of the incredible cult known as "Practical Psychology." It has given rise to a number of religious groups in which God equals mind equals love equals beauty equals happiness equals it ain't goin' to rain no more. This sort of thing appeals to nitwits with a smattering of education and a craving for some self-centered philosophy which will permit them to ignore facts . . .

The key lies in Dr. Menninger's phrase "in some measure." Our mind *can* control itself "in some measure." It is to that measure, however small, that we must address ourselves if we wish to be less depressed.

This does not apply to a persistent, pervasive depression that affects everything we do. Then it is best to see a psychoanalyst. Anyone who advises otherwise is not being wise or kind. We cannot laugh or talk ourselves out of the depression that keeps us in a black mood much of the time. Or causes us to drink too heavily, or work too hard, or not work hard enough, or suffer sleepless nights.

But if depressions are a sometime thing and allow us to function as others do yet still disturb us, there are a number of ways we can help ourselves better to understand how to fight despair when we feel its icy touch.

KEEP ACTIVE, KEEP INTERESTS ALIVE

You cannot ask someone else to put you in a good mood when you feel depressed. This is not the responsibility of anyone other than yourself. Those who depend on someone else for the tenor of their moods are apt to remain unhappy.

What can you do when you feel low in spirits? Some practical things may help. What they are depends on your interests.

There is the old but still valuable advice for a woman to go out and buy a new hat. A recent sentiment on a cover of *Vogue* told the women of America, "Happiness is a new fur coat."

Dr. Menninger asked each member of his class in mental hygiene at Washburn College to describe the method he found most effective in dispelling depression. The replies included the following panaceas:

Take a brisk walk.

Read Shelley and Keats.

Reread an old favorite book.

Read something funny or go to a funny show.

Think to myself that I mustn't take life too seriously.

Work so hard that it is impossible to think of anything else.

Go downtown and look at people and things.

Play hockey or tennis, and dance.

Sleep it away.

Talk things over with some friend who understands.

Put on good clothes and go somewhere.

Play it out on the piano or victrola.

Try to make everybody think I'm feeling good, and pretty soon I am.

"Cuss" it out.

Reason it out in solitude.

Go hunting all by myself.

Start "building air-castles in Spain."

Drive an automobile fast and furiously on a lonely road.

Get with people who are absolutely happy and carefree.

Remember that tomorrow is another day.

In connection with attempts to cure a depression, Dr. Menninger cited the following news story, which satirically hits the heights, or rather depths, in attempted "cures" (unconscious, of course):

TO CURE "BLUES"

Jap Miner Gives That as Reason for Slaying Six Women

Weirdest Murder Mystery in Japan's History Solved

Nagasaki, Japan, June 23 (by mail to United Press)—The weirdest murder mystery in the history of Japan has been solved with the confession of Tokichi Hori, coal miner, that he killed six women and ate part of their flesh.

The six mysterious deaths of women presented the same puzzle—in each case a large piece of flesh had been cut from the victim's right leg. All were killed near the coal mines.

Admitting the murders, Hori confessed he consumed the flesh because of a belief that only this could cure him of melancholia, which affected him for years. He stated that he had served ten years in prison for a similar crime, and since he was released he sought the same cannibalistic remedy every time melancholia possessed him.

This gruesome story certainly bears out the theory of Freud and Abraham, that depression starts with the oral stage in infancy when the baby is frustrated, becomes angry, wants to eat up his mother (particularly her breast), feels guilty, then depressed. The Japanese coal miner's murder of the six women, then his cannibalism, is a regression to the earliest level of life outside the womb. His hunger for his mother's breast appears so intense and his rage at her so devastating that nothing in life could ever satisfy his craving to literally incorporate her, thus unconsciously both destroying her and preserving her within. Incidentally, we might surmise that it was no accident that he always chose the right leg, in that it may have symbolized her right breast, the one at which he was suckled. A rigid leg, also, to the unconscious may symbolize the penis (primitive peoples often ate the penis of a conquered enemy to gain his strength), perhaps the imagined penis of his mother, for children are likely, before they know the facts of life, to suppose their mother has a penis just like the one their father possesses. They are usually pained and uncomfortable to discover she has not, for this arouses their fears of castration.

Incidentally, although the Japanese coal miner *literally* ate women as he may have wished to devour his mother as a baby, this wish may partially explain why some overeat when they are depressed. Food represents to them the mother of infancy. It is as though by eating they can once again feel comforted and loved. At the same time, the act of devouring satisfies the angry feelings within.

Keeping active is one way of thwarting depression (but not as directly active as the Japanese coal miner!). We can go to parties, play sports, join organizations whose aims we believe important, take part in the work of professional societies.

We can do things to raise self-esteem, for in depression, ego is at a low ebb. Self-esteem is different from narcissism, although it starts out as part of the narcissistic drive. The person who remains infantilely narcissistic is selfish, self-indulgent, spoiled. Self-respect stems from achievement and control of selfish impulses in the interest of earning the love of others.

Some find that if they take particular care in how they dress and look, this helps raise self-esteem. The image we present to the world tells what we think of ourselves. When we feel depressed we are apt not to take pains to look chic.

It is important not to blame others for our depression but to know it comes out of ourselves. Only by understanding we are responsible can we successfully battle depression. We can try to become aware of some of the purposes depression may be serving in our lives. We may be seeking such gratifications as attention, sympathy, affection, all noble needs to be fulfilled, but not at great cost to our character. Depression seldom brings what we really want—love.

We should be careful not to use depression as a kind of "mental blackmail," in the words of Dr. Joost Meerloo. Every show of suffering by a depressed person aims at others sharing the burden of pain, he says. The depressed person describes ad infinitum all the injustices he has suffered in an effort to arouse pity and compassion. Dr. Meerloo points out that this provocation is evidence of psychic masochism shown by those whom Dr. Edmund Bergler called "the injustice collectors." These people seek suffering by collecting to their bosom every injustice they can find.

We should ask ourselves if perhaps part of us is afraid to be happy. Some may use depression as a defense against happiness, according to Harold Greenwald.[2] He tells of a very depressed young woman who would come to his office, sit stiffly almost like a catatonic and, when she spoke, talk in jerky sentences.

One day she said, "Well. Went to a party last Saturday. Got drunk."

"How did it feel?" he asked.

"Felt happy," she replied.

"Maybe that's your real self." He intended the comment somewhat as a joke. "Maybe your depression is a defense against happiness."

"That's as good a theory as I've heard," she said earnestly.

"Why do you say that?" He realized his theory was not to be treated jokingly.

"If you're happy, you're an adult. Then you have to do things expected of an adult," she said.

Dr. Greenwald points out this may be one reason for depression. Some do not want to grow up and assume the responsibilities of adults.

"They are afraid to be happy, and what it entails," he says. "Take the business man who is afraid to admit business is good because he fears then it won't get better. Or the fear of success that haunts some writers or actors

It's as though if you're happy, there's no place to go but down."

He explains further:

A defense against happiness is really a defense against responsibility. The happy person is expected to be productive. The depressive uses his unhappiness to prevent the world from asking him to assume mature responsibility. How can you ask a poor, tortured, unhappy, sad, dejected child to do anything?

In addition, the depressive has an easy way of expressing hostility. The depressed person seems to be saying, "Look how I'm suffering and it's your fault." In this way he punishes us by making us feel guilt for his unhappiness and, at the same time, prevents us from expressing our anger by telling us how much he is suffering.

Depression may be a reaction, among other things, to not being able to feel, according to Dr. Ralph M. Crowley, past president of the American Academy of Psychoanalysis, in a special interview. Some who lack the capacity to feel deeply, upon observing others able to express emotions, may become depressed.

He mentions lack of self-esteem as a cause of depression. "When a person feels he is falling short as an individual, how can he feel he has any right to assert anything, including his anger? He thinks he has no right even to *feel* anger."

Dr. Crowley comments:

I don't think the last word has been said about depression. One has to take into account not only the instinctual drives that are not faced or allowed into awareness but the larger picture. This includes high expectations about the self which one cannot possibly meet but which cannot be given up because they are linked to previous experiences and identifications with significant people. And because they relate to one's need to be loved and esteemed.

He gives an example of how a past experience related to self-esteem could be one cause of depression. A woman in analysis said that when she was two years old, her mother took her and her older brother to the seashore to drown them, then changed her mind. Several years later her mother told her this, saying, "I saved you." But the girl was not deceived. She realized that what her mother saved her from was her mother's own impulse to drown her. A mother who wishes to drown her child makes that child feel worthless, indeed, and arouses murderous feelings in return within the child.

FATHOM CAUSES OF DEPRESSION

Would that overcoming a depression could be accomplished by a dose of asafoetida. This was a liquid occasionally given in the old days by the family doctor when called in to calm a hysterical soul. It was a liquid so foul-smelling and evil-tasting that the patient usually preferred to give up his hysteria than to swallow additional asafoetida.

But it helps to become aware that we may have *unreal* causes for depression as well as *real* ones. One woman went through two years of analysis before she was able to face the fact that she was depressed. She had spent years criticizing her mother as the depressed one.

"I'm never going to be a sorrowful old woman like *her*," she kept insisting.

One day she said to the analyst, "My God, I am just starting to realize in what a depression I've been all my life. I've concealed it from myself and others. Go-go-go, I told myself. But underneath it was die-die-die."

She had spent her days in endless, aimless action as a newspaper reporter, dashing all over the world. When she gave up her newspaper career to marry and raise children, she still kept on the go, the social go, an endless round of dinners and cocktail parties. But underneath the frenetic activity, she felt life was hopeless.

By facing some of the hidden causes of her depression, she was able to slow down, to know there was nothing dreadful in her past from which to run away. She had been afraid of her tremendous rage, afraid of admitting it to herself, much less expressing it by word or deed. As she could understand her reasons for anger (some real, some unreal) and uncover fantasies that had driven her so desperately, she lost her depression.

BE AWARE OF ANGER

It is most important when depressed to know that you may be angry at something, or someone. You may be using the depression to hide from yourself a rage you are not prepared to admit.

It is a rage that may be sparked by an event of the moment, such as someone snubbing you or failing to show up at a promised time. Or you may not know what is troubling you. All you know is that you have the feeling of starving to death emotionally and not being able to feed the self.

So, you eat yourself up, in a sense, when you would really like to be chewing up somebody else (literally, in the unconscious). Your psychic hunger is out of childhood and will not be appeased until its true sources become clear.

If you are very depressed, you may blame someone in your current life, but nobody other than the important parents of childhood can have such a shattering impact, one that echoes through the years. What is important in depression, as Freud pointed out, is the childhood wish to get even with (which means murder) the parent for some real or imagined wrong, or to murder the brother or sister who dared to be born and take away what little love there was, plus the lasting guilt over such forbidden wishes.

We probably have to realize, as Freud kept pointing out, that we pay a price for civilization. We have to hold back on our aggressive and sexual feelings, learn to accept a certain amount of frustration in both. This may cause depression at times.

One woman, in telling her analyst about the inhibited years of her adolescence and young womanhood, when she lived a chaste, puritanical life, complained, "When I

think of all that I missed, I could weep. And when I
think that, on marrying, I was suddenly supposed to
enjoy sex, to be free in bed, it was a farce. Yet I know
this is the price we pay for being civilized. Would I
prefer living in jungle days when people had sex all over
the place and killed anyone they hated? No. I'd rather
live now and pay the price. Even though it seems so sad
and wasteful of one's self in a way."

Being wanton sexually is no cure for depression, as
many have found out. The sexually promiscuous person
is just as depressed after escape into sex. He uses sex as a
release from anxiety rather than a shared pleasure with
someone he loves.

Also, in promiscuity anger is likely to invade the sexual feelings, anger unrecognized. Unless you are aware of
your anger and its true targets, the parents of childhood,
you cannot be sexually free. The recent book *The Boston
Strangler,* by Gerold Frank, presents a dramatic example
of how hate and sensuality become fused and confused if
love and tenderness are not present, so that what comes
out is rape and murder.

Awareness of anger is not a matter of age. It is never
too late to do something about depression, provided your
wish is strong enough. Nor is it too early to start, if the
wish is there.

Drugs tend to bury awareness deeper although temporarily they relieve depression. There is little controversy about the use of drugs for the severely depressed
person who has been able to leave a mental hospital,
temporary though the effect of the drugs may be. There is
general agreement that drugs are preferable to electroshock or insulin therapy.

But there is controversy about their use to relieve
depression in the less emotionally disturbed, the so-called
neurotic. Most psychoanalysts will not permit their patients to take drugs. They prefer that the insomnia, the
anxiety, the depression, be worked through on the couch.
There are instances, though, where someone who is quite
depressed, through the use of drugs will become more
accessible to the deeper therapy and will shortly be able

to give up the crutch of drugs. There seems to be no one answer for everyone. The individual case must be judged in all its aspects.

Tranquilizing drugs are used to control such emotional conditions as anxiety, anger and nervousness. In general, major tranquilizers, such as Compazine, Mellaril and Thorazine, are prescribed for psychosis. Minor tranquilizers, such as Equanil, Librium and Miltown, are used for neurotic reactions or tension due to a feeling of being under excessive pressure.

The anti-depressant drugs are used to ease depression, intense grief or sadness. They include such products as Elavil, Tofranil and Marplan.

Drugs are prescribed to enable someone to function more freely and feel more at ease. But they may have other effects which are not therapeutic, and such side effects should be taken into account (blurred vision, dizziness, constipation and dry mouth, and in extreme cases, skin rash, coma or confusion, liver disease or convulsions). One main hazard is dependency on the drug, which prevents the user from ever facing the psychic conflicts that are causing his tension or sleeplessness.

A study of the effect of drugs on severely depressed persons has been conducted for the past three years at The Sheppard and Enoch Pratt Hospital in Towson, Maryland, one of the nation's leading private psychiatric hospitals. It is one of ten mental hospitals taking part in a collaborative study of five hundred patients sponsored by the Psychopharmacology Division of the National Institute of Mental Health.

If a patient on admission shows a significant degree of depression as noted on a standardized rating scale drawn up by the National Institute of Mental Health, he is included in the project. The scale consists of such criteria as: "says he feels blue; talks of feeling helpless, hopeless or worthless; complains of loss of interest; may wish he were dead; reports crying spells; looks sad; cries easily; speaks in a sad voice; appears slowed down; lacking in energy; insomnia, lack of appetite, difficulty concentrating or remembering."

A series of ratings are made over a seven-week period, during which time the patient is given medication, either chlorpromazine or imipramine, or a placebo (a pill or injection without drugs, usually containing sugar). The study is still in progress, since one-year follow-ups are made on all patients.

In summing up the preliminary results, Dr. Robert W. Gibson, medical director of the hospital, says, in a special interview, "I am left with the impression that the drugs do have some effectiveness, but we do not know for precisely what kinds of depressions they are most helpful and in just what way they help the patient.

"Another impression that we developed concerns the ability of trained observers to judge what kind of medication a given patient is receiving. As a part of this study, the observers were asked to judge which drug they felt the patient was receiving. [It should be noted that chlorpromazine and imipramine were given in fairly high doses, probably more than any doctor would give on an outpatient basis.] Although it was possible to judge at a better than chance rate which patients were receiving drugs, the predictions were not a great deal better than chance. When it came to determining whether a patient was getting chlorpromazine or getting imipramine, the ratings were only about chance. This is a rather startling finding. Chlorpromazine is one of the so-called tranquilizers, and imipramine is one of the so-called antidepressants. As you read certain case reports, you see all sorts of very refined statements about how one of these drugs will do such and such, and another will do such and such. People talk about very specific target symptoms, yet here we find a large number of trained observers throughout ten hospitals who were unable to distinguish between these drugs. This leads me to be very skeptical of the individual case reports on drugs that are given by people who study just a small number of patients."

He also points out that in trying to judge whether a patient was receiving a given drug, the trained observers took side reactions, such as blurred vision and dryness of mouth, into account, which, he says, "in the dosage as given I would have thought would have made it very easy to tell what a patient was receiving." However, "just to show how far off one can go, one patient was removed from the study for an intractable side reaction and it turned out that the patient was on a placebo."

One thing about the study that "is most impressive," according to Dr. Gibson, "has been the large number of diagnostic categories of patients able to qualify for this study. All patients had to show was what one might call a moderately severe depression, and yet we had patients of a wide variety of diagnosis in all ages ranging from sixteen to seventy. Thus we see that depression is hardly a single disease entity when it is judged by these characteristics."

He noted another problem that relates to depression. A patient may be very depressed upon entering the hospital, then improve. Dr. Gibson explains, "Admission to a hospital in some cases takes the patient out of a stressful situation and may often lead to marked improvement; in other cases it may lead to an increase in the symptomatology, particularly if the patient experiences the hospitalization as a serious loss of meaningful relationships.

"The planned environment of most hospitals tends to gratify many of the dependency needs which depressed patients seem to have, and may therefore lead to a rapid improvement. The giving of some kind of medication even if it is a placebo also gratifies dependency needs and may be helpful to the patient in relieving his symptoms. As a matter of fact, some people have said that one could make a fairly good case that a placebo could be considered as an effective agent in the treatment of depression, since it generally leads to improvement in about 30 to 40 per cent of the cases. Also, in most hospitals there is some kind of specific individual treatment program going on. Certainly this is true of Sheppard Pratt. In our study we have continued to offer all phases of our treatment program as well as the drugs. Thus one finds it very difficult to tell just what is leading to the improvement of a patient. In other words, if a patient is admitted with problems, and promptly started on some kind of medication, there is good chance that the patient will improve rather rapidly, but how can one be sure that it is due to the drug?

"The study in which Sheppard Pratt is participating is an attempt to overcome some of these difficulties. By collecting a large series of cases, something over five hundred through the collaboration of these ten hospitals, it has been possible to get patients with many different diagnoses, many differences in age, and to study them in a systematic way. To my knowledge, no study of this type has ever been conducted before, even though much has been written about these drugs and they have been given to literally millions of people and probably tens of millions of dollars spent on them."

In the case of the man on the street and drugs, he has to trust his physician as to when to use them, and the dosage. Perhaps it would be pertinent to quote the advice given physicians by the Committee on Alcoholism and Addiction of the American Medical Association.[3]

The committee points out that the "extra cautious" physician is the key in limiting the use of drugs such as opiates. He is also the key in limiting "less potent narcotics." Vast differences in properties and effects of drugs, however, make it difficult to ensure that every physician is aware of the potentials for misuse of barbiturates and amphetamines. The reduced hazards seem to make the physician less cautious than he should be.

The committee lists four general patterns of abuse by patients of barbiturates and urges physicians to become familiar with these patterns: (a) some patients seek sedation to escape emotional distress; (b) some appear to enjoy the "paradoxical excitory reaction which occurs after tolerance development"; (c) others use barbiturates to counteract the effects of stimulant drugs; and (d) still others use alcohol to "potentiate" [make more powerful] the barbiturates, "and this is very dangerous."

Recognition of the potential abuser is only part of the physician's responsibility, according to the committee. It stated frankly, "The ground work for the patient's drug abuse is often established by therapeutic misuse by the physician." It cited four situations that constitute misuse by the doctor:

a. A physician accedes to a patient's demand for increased dosage because the lesser dosage has failed to ease the symptoms, and the physician fails to recognize that the request itself indicates increasing tolerance for the drug, leading toward dependence.

b. By failing to elicit a complete medical history or establish a definite diagnosis prior to administering the barbiturate, the physician may overlook a history of dependence on drugs, or emotional instability predisposing the patient to dependence on the drugs.

c. In spite of repeated warnings, some physicians still write refillable prescriptions. This practice is "extremely dangerous" and "is indulged in only by physicians ignorant of or willing to ignore the hazards involved."

d. "Ironically," some physicians attempting to prevent barbiturate dependence by substituting a non-barbiturate sedative merely supplant one form of dependence with another "equally dangerous one." A 1965 survey at the University of Kentucky Medical Center Psychiatric Ward showed that of 132 consecutive admissions of general psychiatric patients, five were dependent on glutethimide, which is supposedly harmless, while only three were dependent on barbiturates. Apparently physicians in that area had "frequently" substituted glutethimide for barbiturates, the committee said.

It recommended that stimulants or depressant drugs be used only for prescribed periods and for specific medical purposes. These would include controlling the appetite, combating depression, reducing insomnia or "enhancing the action of analgesic medicines" (those that relieve pain).

Even when there is justification for medical use of amphetamines, the physician must recognize that the stimulant's efficacy in helping the patient achieve a "time-limited goal" could predispose him to look upon the drug as a solution for future problems and lead to eventual drug abuse, the committee pointed out.

The widespread use of drugs was condemned by Dr.

Joseph Franklin Montague, president of the American Medical Authors Association.[4] He wrote:

There may be some who damn officials now so energetic in attempting to correct the situation, but I believe that every thinking physician is giving a silent vote of approval to the new era of drug appraisal. Eventually, the public will find that this has been the greatest step forward in preventive medicine since the invention of vaccine.

NOBODY CAN COMPLETELY ESCAPE MOODS

We can never expect to be wholly without the feeling of depression as it occurs in the occasional mood. We need it, just as we need every other emotion we possess. If we think we are going to live without it, this is a remnant of the childhood belief in magic.

The capacity to become depressed lies in us the moment we start to breathe. We have to learn to bear a certain amount of depression so that when there occur the inevitable losses, disappointments and frustrations of life, we meet them with the proper emotion.

The mastering of depression enables us to accept more easily what otherwise would be overwhelming tragedy and also leads to greater maturity. As we accept some measure of depression, we accept some measure of reality, renouncing much of the magic of childish wishes.

"Psychotic depression is the outcome of a failure to experience and master the depression inevitable in developmental crises," says Dr. Elizabeth R. Zetzel.[5]

She explains, "Acute separation anxiety and explosive rage often precede the emergence of genuine sadness or depression. This affect [feeling] marks the first decisive step toward achieving the passive component of psychic maturity."

Substantial success "leads to the capacity to contain or tolerate depression without serious ego regression." Once achieved, passive acceptance must be followed by "active mastery," which makes easier the development of feelings of relating to others, learning and "ultimately the capacity for happiness."

In other words, we have to learn how to "contain" a slight amount of depression to be happy. The more we can accept that a little depression is part of reality, the less depressed we are apt to be.

We will have taken the early depressive feelings in our stride if we received a fair share of love as we grew up. The one who has been emotionally healthy as a child can cope with the recurrence of mild feelings of depression. He will not sink into a deep depression when he feels frustrated. He accepts a certain amount of frustration as appropriate to living and puts his energy into something other than anger, or puts his anger into such constructive uses as working or playing golf or tennis or bridge or poker.

As Dr. Helene Deutsch wrote, when you understand the self, you forgive the self, but then you also find there is really nothing to forgive. You come to know that depression, if it has been persistent, is the useless fight you have waged against the phantoms of the past, which led to the painful patterns of the present.

WHEN PSYCHOANALYSIS CAN HELP

If those phantoms and patterns are too persistent and too powerful, it is possible psychoanalysis will help those who cannot help themselves through "will power," or, if you prefer that other cliché, by "pulling themselves up out of it by their own bootstraps."

Actually, depression is apt to be part of every neurosis, although in some it stands out more sharply than others. How could it be otherwise? Depression follows guilt and guilt is usually possessed in abundance by those unable to feel happy. As the guilt and what it shadows—the hostility—is faced and eased, the depression automatically disappears, as does our shadow when the sun is shining and we turn in another direction.

A number of psychoanalysts have reported successful treatment of depressions. This is one measure of the success of psychoanalysis in alleviating depression. Another is the number of men and women who have been analyzed and who attest to the loss of a once-persistent depression. They realized it had both real and unreal causes, and that they had used it as a way of not facing feelings they believed shameful, humiliating and hateful.

One woman went into analysis because she could not shake a depression that was keeping her home from work. She found she had good reason to feel depressed. Her mother had died when she was two, and this above all else will leave a child devastated, as Dr. Bowlby and others have shown.

But her depression also had unreal causes, in that, over the years, she had despised a stepmother whom she thought of as a cruel woman but who, in reality, had given her a good home and as much affection as the motherless child would accept.

As this woman could understand that her father had been far happier remarried, and as a result she, too, had been happier, and as she could face her natural feelings of jealousy toward her stepmother, her anger, guilt and depression lifted.

While depressed psychotic patients are far more difficult to treat, there are those who have had success, although treatment takes much longer. The patient has to have a deep enough wish to get better and the therapist must possess deep compassion and unending patience.

Psychotherapy is difficult but not impossible with the manic-depressive personality, according to Dr. Robert Gibson, mentioned earlier in this chapter as medical director of The Sheppard and Enoch Pratt Hospital. When he was on the staff of Chestnut Lodge, in Rockville, Maryland, he reported on the treatment of patients there. [6, 7]

The chief problem with such patients was to break through barriers and establish "a communicative relationship," according to Dr. Gibson. Various methods were advocated for achieving this breakthrough, many of which were related to the personality of the therapist. Dr.

Gibson comments, "Regardless of the specific manner of approach, a general attitude of active involvement with the patient was thought desirable, in contrast to the more passive attitudes appropriate in treating neurotics."

However, it was agreed by all that the active involvement must also carry with it an equally active refusal to be manipulated into the position of meeting the patient's dependency needs. Should this occur, the patient will merely be repeating his pre-psychotic pattern with a new object. There is also the danger that the therapist, having drifted into the position of being the source of the patient's dependent gratifications, will eventually free himself from this entanglement by withdrawing from or rejecting the patient.

He points out, "In our experience, the dangers of suicide were greatest when the patient felt unrelated; even a hostile integration with another seemed to lessen this risk . . . Even negative responses to his destructive attitudes or his manipulative attempts may be usefully expressed to him if they are genuinely and warmly felt."

The prevention of suicide is now a matter of world concern. The International Association for Suicide Prevention has been established in Vienna (fit place, as the home of Freud, who revolutionized our thinking about the cause of suicide and depression in general). This is an organization through which individuals and agencies from different countries can exchange experiences and information about suicide, with the aim of preventing it. The new organization has as general secretary Norman L. Farberow, head of the Los Angeles Suicide Prevention Center, the only one of its kind in the United States. It was set up in 1958 under a U. S. Public Health Service grant as a demonstration project with three purposes: to learn about suicide in order to develop and test out effective suicide prevention methods; to establish a community suicide prevention service using these methods; and to continue a program of research into the nature, causes and prevention of suicide.

The National Institute of Mental Health, which sponsored the above project, also has given a five-year grant of $850,000 to the Henry Phipps Psychiatric Clinic of the Johns Hopkins School of Medicine to establish a curriculum, recruit teaching personnel and provide fellowships for training in dealing with suicide. The director of this project is Dr. Seymour Perlin, professor of psychiatry at Johns Hopkins.

A "Crisis Club" has been set up by the department of child psychiatry at the Cedars-Sinai Medical Center, Mt. Sinai Division, in Los Angeles. One aim of the group therapy given to twenty-two suicidal women has been to reduce their destructive feelings.

Dr. Sandor Lorand, who has written extensively about depression, in discussing neurotic depression emphasizes that its treatment should center on the person's learning not to be afraid to express his anger, anger that has possibly been repressed for a lifetime. For this anger, and the subsequent guilt turned on the self, has caused the suffering and depression.

How is this achieved on the couch? According to Dr. Lorand, in a special interview:

Interpretation, intellectual understanding, is not enough. The crucial thing is for the patient to learn by experience not to be afraid, no longer to feel intimidated and to be able to ventilate his stormy, aggressive feelings in the analyst's office. This has to be a real emotional experience, one of flesh and bones and blood. Not an intellectual, cerebral affair.

The depressed person is "getting even" with his parents of childhood, Dr. Lorand says. He cites the song "You Made Me What I Am Today, I Hope You're Satisfied" as the theme song of the depressed person as he proclaims to the world, "My parents made me what I am today. Let them suffer."

During psychoanalysis patients will lose their depression only as they can express the early fury, as well as their love for and dependency on the analyst. They must be encouraged to speak of all their thoughts and feelings but particularly not to hold back on the aggressive ones.

"The depressed person never dares express his aggressive feelings but swallows them and becomes depressed," says Dr. Lorand. "Then comes the depression, partly as a revenge—tormenting the family or those near him—partly a self-punishment for tormenting those around him."

Psychoanalysis is bound to be a frustrating experience, Dr. Lorand points out. At first, the patient is, in a sense, seduced by the analyst's kindness and attempt to help. In the beginning or positive phase, the patient loves and admires "the big helper." But then, not getting what he wants, "love, love, love, for all depressed persons are insatiable in their need for love," the patient will feel frustrated. He must be able to ventilate his rage at this frustration, as he once wished to do with his parents but was afraid.

In order to be able to accept the abuse and aggressiveness which is inevitably turned against the analyst, who becomes a substitute for all authorities who instilled the original fear and rebellion in the patient as a child, adolescent and adult, the analyst himself must be well analyzed so he does not take the patient's anger personally, Dr. Lorand warns. The analyst must guard against showing any negative reaction to provocations the patient will put forth. The analyst must know that only through the ventilation of aggression will the patient slowly learn not to be afraid. Through expressing fear and rage in this person-to-person encounter, the patient has the experience, probably for the first time in his life, of being with someone who understands him, tolerates him in spite of his anger and can help him.

"Thus he is no longer afraid, can express his rage without feeling guilty, doesn't have to swallow his feelings and no longer needs to feel depressed," says Dr. Lorand.

The treatment of depressed persons is difficult because the patient is likely to be afraid for a long time to express anger, Dr. Lorand maintains. Instead, he wants to run

away, "every day." It is up to the analyst to understand
that such a reaction is natural, that the patient is afraid
not of the analyst but of his own aggression.

Can depression be "cured"? Dr. Lorand calls "cure" a
matter of the degree of help. He explains:

There is no 100 percent cure in medical treatment. If you
break a leg, a surgeon can help by setting it but that leg will
always be weaker, more sensitive to the weather, than the
other leg. This is also true if we think in terms of strengthening
a crippled psyche. There is no 100 percent cure. If we can
give 70 percent help, that is a great help, amounting to 100
percent. If we give 50 percent help, that is very satisfactory.
Even 25 percent enables the person to live more happily.

He says further:

The aim of psychoanalysis is to help someone function
better in three main areas; the work area, the social area (to
become a more sociable member of society) and the pleasure
area (sexual functioning). The aim of analysis is to make
people feel happier. To what degree they feel happier depends
on a number of things. First, how emotionally ill the person
has been and how much his sickness is reduced, his emotional
burden eased. Second, the age, for it is easier to establish
nearly normal functioning in a young person than one over
fifty, although this does not mean someone fifty or sixty
cannot be analyzed. Third, on the personality, capability and
elasticity of the analyst.

Dr. Edith Jacobson, who has also treated the severely
depressed person with marked success, told of a woman
who had never undergone any therapy, although from the
age of sixteen to twenty-eight she suffered severe depressions for which she was regularly put into a mental
hospital.[8] When she was twenty-eight, her father died,
and half a year later she had her first love affair. After
two years without any relapse into illness, she got married. Despite tragic events in her life, such as the suicide
of her mother and her best woman friend, she never

again suffered a breakdown, although at the age of forty-seven she did have mild depressions and swings of mood.

Commented Dr. Jacobson, "If life can achieve so much, analysis should be able to do even more."

The average man or woman does not go to a psycho-analyst when he feels a momentary depression. He knows it will pass and life will continue as before.

Most of us do not need to live either with Job's philosophy of despair or the hedonist's "Eat, drink and be merry, for tomorrow we die." We are aware reality lies somewhere in between.

We try to find a temperate trail, knowing life will hold moments that are sad as well as moments that are happy. We try not to let the sad moments take on darkness from the past.

Notes

1

1. Grinker, Roy S., M.D.; Miller, Julian, M.D.; Sabshin, Melvin, M.D.; Nunn, Robert, M.D. and Nunnally, Jum C., *The Phenomena of Depressions,* Paul B. Hoeber, Inc., Medical Division of Harper & Brothers, 1961.
2. Ruddick, Bruce, M.D., "Colds and Respiratory Introjection," in *The International Journal of Psycho-analysis,* Vol. 44, Part 2, 1963.
3. "The Common Cold and Depression," paper delivered by Dr. Merl M. Jackel at the fall meeting of the American Psychoanalytic Association, December 16, 1967, New York City.
4. "The Emotional Basis of Illness," paper delivered by Dr. Augustus Gibson at a meeting for physicians sponsored by the Schering Corporation, March 30, 1967, in New York City.
5. Report on the history of one thousand patients treated for seven years at the Headache Clinic of Montefiore Hospital and Medical Center, New York, by Dr. Arnold P. Friedman.
6. Talks delivered by narcotics authorities and county executives at a meeting in December 1967 of educators and county officials in White Plains, Westchester County, New York.
7. Studies conducted under the direction of Dr. Melvin L. Selzer, Associate Professor of Psychiatry at the University of Michigan Medical School, Ann Arbor.
8. Menninger, Karl, *Man Against Himself,* Harcourt, Brace & Company, 1938.
9. Address delivered by George R. Bach at the annual convention of the American Psychological Association, Washington, September 1967.

2

1. Freud, Sigmund, "The Relation of the Poet to Day-Dreaming," *Collected Papers,* Vol. IV, The Hogarth Press, 1925.
2. Ibid.
3. Riviere, Joan, "On the Genesis of a Psychical Conflict in Earliest Infancy," *The International Journal of Psycho-analysis,* Vol. 17, October 1936.

3

1. *The Origins of Psychoanalysis: Sigmund Freud's Letters to Wilhelm Fliess, Drafts and Notes, 1887–1902,* edited by Marie Bonaparte, Anna Freud, Ernst Kris; translated by Eric Mosbacher and James Strachey; Basic Books, 1954.
2. Freud, Sigmund, "Mourning and Melancholia," *Standard Edition of the Complete Psychological Works of Sigmund Freud,* Vol. 14, Hogarth Press and the Institute of Psycho-Analysis, London, 1957.
3. Freud, Sigmund, "Group Psychology and the Analysis of the Ego," *Standard Edition,* Vol. 18, 1957.
4. Stewart, Walter A., M.D., *Psychoanalysis: The First Ten Years,* The Macmillan Company, 1967.
5. Milt, Harry, *The Roots of Suicide,* Merck, Sharp & Dohme, 1966.

4

1. Abraham, Karl, M.D., "Notes on the Psychoanalytical Investigation and Treatment of Manic-Depressive Insanity and Allied Conditions," from *Selected Papers,* Basic Books, 1953.
2. Freud, Sigmund, *The Letters of Sigmund Freud and Karl Abraham, 1907–1926,* edited by Hilda C. Abraham and Ernest L. Freud, Basic Books, 1965.

5

1. Klein, Melanie, *The Psychoanalysis of Children,* Grove Press, 1960.
2. Klein, Melanie, "Mourning and Its Relation to Manic-Depressive States," *The International Journal of Psycho-*

analysis, Vol. 21, Part 2, April 1940. This paper was originally read before the Fifteenth Psycho-analytical Congress in Paris, in 1938.

3. Spitz, René, M.D., *The First Year of Life,* International Universities Press, 1965.

4. Bowlby, John, M.D., "Childhood Mourning and Its Implications for Psychiatry," *The American Journal of Psychiatry,* Vol. 118, No. 6, December 1961. This article was originally The Adolf Meyer Lecture at the 117th Annual Meeting of the American Psychiatric Association in Chicago, May 1961.

5. Mahler, Margaret, M.D., "Notes on the Development of Basic Moods: The Depressive Affect," chapter in *Psychoanalysis—A General Psychology,* 1966.

6. Mahler, Margaret, M.D., "On the Significance of the Normal Separation-Individuation Phase," chapter in the book *Drives, Affects, Behavior,* edited by Max Schur, International Universities Press, Vol. 2, 1966.

7. Jacobson, Edith, M.D., "The Return of the Lost Parent," chapter in *Drives, Affects, Behavior,* edited by Max Schur, International Universities Press, Vol. 2, 1966.

8. Jacobson, Edith, M.D., "The Effect of Disappointment on Ego and Super-Ego Formation in Normal and Depressive Development," *The Psychoanalytic Review,* Vol. 33, No. 2, April 1946.

9. Lorand, Sandor, M.D., "Dynamics and Therapy of Depressive States," *The Psychoanalytic Review,* Vol. 24, No. 4, October 1937.

10. Rado, Sandor, M.D., "The Problem of Melancholia," *The International Journal of Psycho-analysis,* Vol. 19, October 1928.

11. Eidelberg, Ludwig, M.D., *An Outline of a Comparative Pathology of the Neuroses,* International Universities Press, 1954.

12. Eidelberg, Ludwig, M.D., "The Effects of Admonition in Child Training," chapter in *Studies in Psychoanalysis,* International Universities Press, 1952.

13. Gero, Georg, M.D., "The Construction of Depression," *The International Journal of Psycho-analysis,* Vol. 17, October 1936.

14. Fries, Margaret, M.D., "Some Factors in the Development and Significance of Early Object Relationships," *Journal of the American Psychoanalytic Association,* Vol. IX, No. 4, October 1961.

15. Fries, Margaret, M.D., "Mental Hygiene in Pregnancy, Delivery, and the Puerperium," *Mental Hygiene,* Vol. XXV, No. 2. April 1941.
16. Geleerd, Elisabeth R., M.D., "Some Aspects of Ego Vicissitudes in Adolescence," *Journal of the American Psychoanalytic Association,* Vol. IX, No. 3, July 1961.
17. Grotjahn, Martin, M.D., *Beyond Laughter,* McGraw-Hill, 1957.
18. Freud, Anna, *The Psycho-analytical Treatment of Children,* Imago Publishing Co. Ltd., London, 1946.
19. Gralnick, Alexander, M.D., "Marriages Are Made in Heaven," chapter in *The Mind,* Thomas Y. Crowell, 1967. The case originally appeared as a paper, "The Carrington Family: A Psychiatric and Social Study Illustrating the Psychosis of Association or *Folie à Deux,*" in *The Psychiatric Quarterly,* Vol. XVII, April 1943.
20. Olive, Roger O., "The Child-Killing Mother," paper delivered at the Annual Convention of the American Psychological Association in Washington, D.C., September 1967.
21. Spotnitz, Hyman, M.D., *Modern Psychoanalysis of the Schizophrenic Patient,* Grune & Stratton, 1968.
22. Ferenczi, Sandor, M.D., "The Unwelcome Child and His Death Instinct," *The International Journal of Psychoanalysis,* Vol. XX, 1929.
23. Lorand, Sandor, M.D., *The Technique of Psychoanalytic Therapy,* International Universities Press, 1946.
24. Rheingold, Joseph, M.D., *The Fear of Being a Woman,* Grune & Stratton, 1964.
25. Bloch, Dorothy, "Feelings That Kill: The Effect of the Wish for Infanticide in Neurotic Depression," *The Psychoanalytic Review,* Vol. 52, No. 1, Spring 1965.
26. Hoffer, Willi, M.D., "Mouth, Hand and Ego Integration," *Psychoanalytic Study of the Child,* 3-4, 49-56. International Universities Press, Inc., 1949.

6

1. Meerloo, Joost A. M., *Suicide and Mass Suicide,* Grune & Stratton, 1963.
2. Freud, Sigmund, "The Relation of the Poet to Day-Dreaming," *Collected Papers,* Vol. IV, The Hogarth Press, London, 1925.

3. Freud, Sigmund, "Formulations on the Two Principles of Mental Functioning," *Standard Edition*, 12, 1958.

4. Freud, Sigmund, "Introductory Lectures on Psycho-Analysis," *Standard Edition*, 16, 1963.

5. Freud, Sigmund, "Formulations on the Two Principles of Mental Functioning," *Standard Edition*, 3, 1962.

6. Freud, Sigmund, *Leonardo Da Vinci: A Study in Psychosexuality*, Random House, 1947.

7. Sharpe, Ella, "Similar and Divergent Unconscious Determinants Underlying the Sublimations of Pure Art and Pure Science," *The International Journal of Psycho-analysis*, Vol. 16, 1935.

8. Klein, Melanie, *Contributions to Psycho-Analysis, 1921–1945*, McGraw-Hill (paperback), 1964.

9. Markson, John W., M.D., "Writing Out and Through," *American Imago*, Vol. 23, No. 3, Fall 1966.

10. Greenacre, Phyllis, M.D., "The Childhood of the Artist: Libidinal Phase Development and Giftedness," chapter in *The Psychoanalytic Study of the Child*, Vol. XII, 1957.

11. Schneider, Daniel E., M.D., *The Psychoanalyst and the Artist*, International Universities Press, 1950.

12. Hammer, Emanuel F., *Creativity*, Random House, 1961.

13. Kubie, Lawrence S., M.D., *Neurotic Distortion of the Creative Process*, The Noonday Press, 1961.

14. Weissman, Philip, M.D., *Creativity in the Theatre*, Basic Books, 1957.

7

1. Lewin, Bertram D., M.D., *The Psychoanalysis of Elation*, W. W. Norton, 1950.

2. Freud, Sigmund, "Humour," *Collected Papers*, Vol. V, Hogarth Press, Ltd., London, 1934.

3. Freud, Sigmund, "Wit and Its Relation to the Unconscious," in *The Basic Writings of Sigmund Freud*, Modern Library, 1938.

4. Grotjahn, Martin, M.D., *Beyond Laughter*, McGraw-Hill, 1957.

5. Reik, Theodor, *Jewish Wit*, Gamut Press, 1962.

8

1. Lorand, Rhoda, *Love, Sex and the Teenager*, The Macmillan Company, 1965.

2. Green, Maurice R., M.D., talk on "Depression in Adolescence," given at the American Psychiatric Association meeting, Fall 1965.

3. Braaten, Leif J.; Darling, C. Douglas, M.D., "Suicidal Tendencies Among College Students," *The Psychiatric Quarterly*, Vol. 36, No. 4, 1962.

4. Rangell, Leo, M.D., speaking at a "Seminar for Science Writers, on Psychoanalysis," at the Fall Meeting of the American Psychoanalytic Association, December 14, 1967, New York City.

5. Freud, Anna, "Adolescence," *The Psychoanalytic Study of the Child*, Vol. VI, International Universities Press, Inc., 1951.

6. Nicholi, Armand, M.D., speaking at the Annual Meeting of the American Psychiatric Association in Detroit, May 1967.

7. Lorand, Sandor, M.D., "Adolescent Depression," *The International Journal of Psycho-analysis*, Vol. 48, 1967.

8. Szalita, Alberta B., M.D., "Psychodynamics of Disorders of the Involutional Age," chapter in *American Handbook of Psychiatry*, Vol. 3, edited by Silvano Arieti, Basic Books, 1959.

9. Grotjahn, Martin, M.D., "Analytic Psychotherapy with the Elderly," *The Psychoanalytic Review*, Vol. 42, No. 4, October 1955.

10. Goldfarb, Alvin I., M.D., "Psychiatric Disorders of the Aged," *Journal of the American Geriatric Society* (8), 1960.

9

1. Menninger, Karl, M.D., *The Human Mind*, The Literary Guild of America, 1930.

2. Greenwald, Harold, *Emotional Maturity in Love and Marriage*, with Lucy Freeman, Harper & Brothers, 1961.

3. August 1965 issue of the *Journal of the American Medical Association*.

4. Montague, Joseph Franklin, M.D., "The New Style Hypochondriac," *Clinical Medicine*, Vol. 73, September 1966.

5. Zetzel, Elizabeth R., M.D., "Depression and the Incapacity to Bear It," chapter in *Drives, Affects, Behavior*, edited by Max Schur, International Universities Press, Vol. 2, 1966.

6. Gibson, Robert W., M.D., "Psychotherapy of Manic-

Depressive States," *Psychiatric Research Report 17,* American Psychiatric Association, November 1963.

7. Gibson, Robert, M.D.; Cohen, Mabel B., M.D.; and Cohen, Robert A., M.D., "On the Dynamics of the Manic-Depressive Personality," *The American Journal of Psychiatry,* Vol. 115, No. 12, June 1959.

8. Jacobson, Edith, M.D., "Depression: The Oedipus Conflict in the Development of Depressive Mechanisms," *The Psychoanalytic Quarterly,* Vol. XII, No. 4, October 1943.

Index